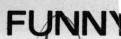

FUNNY BONE

BY

Herb True, Ph.D.

Research Psychologist and Motivation Consultant

Illustrated By
JIM PICKENS

Cover Design
JOHN CERNAK

Typography
KATHY KERR

Editor
BETTY DICK

ASSOCIATE EDITORS

Don Norton — Thelma Howard — Donna Skiles — Bill Dick
Connie Hume — Elaine Lee — Anna Mang — Art Fettig

Published by
American Humor Guild

TABLE OF CONTENTS

INTRODUCTION

Although the "Funnybone" of this book doesn't appear on any medical chart of the human body, it's a very real thing, the site of your unique sense of humor . . . uniquely yours because YOU create it.

Your sense of humor can be improved at almost any age. It begins with "thinking funny". (You grasp a situation, give it a twist round a corner, turn it inside out — and see the funny side of it.) When you "think funny", you take yourself lightly and your job in life seriously. You laugh AT yourself and WITH others, for what they do, NOT what they are.

The above statements represent some of the things we believe about humor.

Who are "we"?

"We" refers to our TEAM, the group of associates who work with me and to whom I have delegated my future. As president of TEAM International, Inc., I present, and have for 20 years, at least 180 programs a year, to a wide variety of business, industrial, government, education, religious, and civic groups, throughout the United States and Canada, in South America, the Carribean, Mexico, and Australia.

One constant item in my presentations is the use of humor as a tactical instrument to inform and inspire, to reinforce concepts, and to demonstrate my long-held belief that learning should be fun — not play, but fun. Typically, the banquet-luncheon presentation contains 70% humor and 30% content, while the impact-workshops and seminars involve 80% content and 20% humor.

Most presentations also utilize original, multi-colored graphics to reinforce the special subject areas of creativity, motivation, selling, management, communication, leadership, love, and humor.

Our own specialists create, and we purchase from writers, such material as one-liners, jokes, quips, and stories that are woven into the presentations in vignette form.

In addition, some thirty "uniforms", as we call them — rather than "costumes" — add another element of humor and provide continuity for appropriate themes. For example, I wear a king's robe to emphasize that "the customer is king" and a prisoner's stripes to stress the concept that we create our own prisons, thereby limiting our talents and abilities.

Helping me to build and deliver these presentations are such TEAM members as Research Director, Don Norton; Humor Director, Betty Dick; Program Manager, Thelma Howard; Art Director, Elaine Lee; Illustrators, Jim Pickens and John Cernak; and Director of Records and Cassettes, Donna Skiles.

I

A lot has happened since our first humor book, "Laugh Oil", was published in 1968. We would like to share with you some elements of our philosophy, as it has developed. Most discussions of humor start with defining it. Over the years, humanity has used humor without quite knowing what it is. Even modern technology can't pinpoint it. When researchers talk about a sense of humor, they use words like "fragile", "elusive", "intangible". They say it's easier to recognize than to explain.

Never-the-less, we value this "sixth sense" of humor in our associates, our friends, our families. We appreciate and admire it in our national leaders. We observe that the winners of the world count on humor — to lighten the load and lead the way to a more efficient, productive, successful life.

In part, a sense of humor may be hard to define because we confuse humor with comedy or wit. Your sense of humor does react to wit, comedy, jokes, satire, and irony. Each tickles your "Funnybone", causing you to express amusement, joy, laughter, or mirth.

Traditionally, the "rude shock", sarcasm, and ridicule are considered hurtful forms of humor. Sarcasm is satire gone wild with bitterness.

Ridicule, however, seems to be playing a new role. It's my observation that it's use is more prevalent than in the days when I began speaking. The difference? Helpful ridicule contains elements of honesty and an implied compliment. For instance: "Gee, I wish cheap clothes looked good on me." It's required that either the clothes really aren't cheap, or you and the person you compliment wear clothes in the same price range — and he looks better in them.

Above all, a SENSE of humor is at once broader and more delicate than any of the forms of or reaction to humor itself. Instead of merely a propensity to laugh at jokes or smile at satire, it's a philosophy, a way of looking at and responding to life. A sense of humor lends proportion, balance, and flexibility to living.

It's never too early — or too late — to develop your "sixth sense". When babies really laugh for the first time, they're no longer infants. They're children. But some "babies" wait till they're middle-aged or older to mature. We really grow up — the day we learn to laugh at ourselves.

Like most forms of behavior, a sense of humor is learned. Because laughter is contagious, we learn from others how to laugh. Some scarred children have never seen their parents laugh. Yet children thrive on humor and develop a strong sense of it when they're constantly with adults who don't hesitate to show their own sixth sense.

From the long history of humor, we learn some of the things our sense of humor can do for us.

Ancient Romans believed laughter belonged at the banquet table because it aided digestion. They were right. Laughter and other reactions to humor prevent fear and anger, both of which interfere with the digestive process. For general health, modern physicians say humor is the greatest tonic of all.

Early Greeks knew that laughter is the other face of tears. There dramatists expressed this truth with the twin masks of tragedy and comedy. Humor has value when sorrow needs relief, for the best of humor holds elements of compassion and tenderness. We laugh to relieve tensions, to shake off anxieties. The most serious problems can be better solved in a relaxed atmosphere. Humor relaxes.

In medieval times, the jester was often the highest-paid person at court. The jester's humor helped the king carry the burdens and lift the load of ruling the land. In more recent centuries, great leaders from Lincoln to Churchill have turned to a sense of humor in times of crisis.

Mirth is God's medium. When Jesus sojourned on earth, He used humor to express an idea and fix it in the minds of His followers. We speak jokingly of a "wolf in sheep's clothing" — without remembering that this expression comes from His Sermon on the Mount.

The same Sermon is replete with satire and irony. Jesus explained that when people light a candle, they don't put it under a bushel basket; they put it in a candlestick. He advised that, when we give to charity, we shouldn't sound a trumpet, as hypocrites do, and He observed that hypocrites take care to pray publicly, standing on a streetcorner or prominently in the temple.

His listeners must have smiled with a sense of recognition when Jesus inquired, "If a man's son ask bread, would he give him a stone? If he ask a fish, would he give him a serpent?" and "Do men gather grapes of thorns, or herbs of thistles?"

As Jesus showed, a sense of humor can make us more aware of the bigger meaning of life. It reveals our inner selves, so that we can increase our own enjoyment of living and help others recognize us for what we really are. It helps us know and improve ourselves, by conquering arrogance and egotism. It inspires us to cope with difficulties, by dispelling disappointment and dispair.

Currently, there's a theory that, with television and other technological means of communication — such as the canned laughter of the laugh track — people are losing their sense of humor. I don't subscribe to that theory. Among live audiences,

I find a great willingness to accept the philosophy that they can lift their load with laughter.

As for my personal philosophy of humor, I don't look on myself as a story teller. Rather, I hope that my material is short, to the point and making a point, so that the point will be remembered and not be overshadowed by the humor.

I do have strong feelings about platform humor. I aim for a "mad, glad, blend of all cleans, — no dirties."

Although humor dealing with ethnic groups, religion, and politics is considered questionable by some, I take a humorous approach to problems that arise in these areas. But only when I can, for example, tie in the fact that my mother is Irish, quote someone from a particular ethnic group, or relate what I'm saying to myself, my family, my training, or the people in the audience.

I feel this kind of humor is important, since so many cultures — among them, the Irish, Jewish, and Black cultures — have used their sense of humor to help them carry burdens in extremely difficult situations.

One area which I find delicate, concerns humor about women. Much such humor, over the years, has been the kind that degrades, or uses a putdown manner toward women and their physical characteristics. I try to explain that, my kidding about my wife and daughter and women concerns relatively real experiences and isn't meant to be demeaning.

Whatever, the subjects, the jokes, stories, one-liners, quips, and quotes in this book are audience-tested and audience-proved. Our main purpose in publishing "Funnybone" is to share with you the humor that our TEAM has shared with audiences and that those audiences have shared with us. For instance:

The poems included have been given to us by people in our audiences. Unfortunately, we've been unable to track down the names of the poets who wrote these favorite verses. For that, we owe an apology and perhaps an additional apology for our adaptations of the poems, to make them applicable to our presentations.

I've learned from my 15 years' work with the first professional speakers organization, Speakers Associates, that most stories have many parents. Witness the story about two comedians, talking before their act. One said to the other: "If you won't use my Bob Hope jokes, I won't use your Flip Wilson jokes." In this book, I've included some dear old friends and "adopted children", along with material I have sought to make my own.

Since timeliness is a primary factor in our presentations, a book of this sort is hard to do. Although our TEAM has been working for two years, to compile material from our presentations and cassettes and to eliminate "dated" elements wherever possible, you may find that some "Funnybone" humor is current now but won't be in a week, a month, or a year.

Remember that countless switches are possible. The most obvious example related to the widely used political quip, attributed to Will Rogers: "I'm not a member of any organized political party. I'm a Democrat (Republican)."

A complete "thank you" list would be longer than the book. More briefly, I'd like to say thanks to:

My wife Betty Ann and our True Tribe, Robert, Mike, Steve, Jeff, Greg, Nancy, Lisa, and Mary — the willing brunt of and testing ground for many of my stories.

Friends like Joel Bullard, Art Fettig, Bill Gove, Dik Twedt, and all my teachers in Speakers Associates who have endured my practicing nearly all of these stories on them many times, before I attempted using the material in front of an audience.

Outstanding humorists like Mack McGinnis, and Bob Orben, valued long-time friends whose humor services have inspired many timely ideas.

Those 180-plus audiences a year, whose patience and understanding have been of immeasurable help to me.

And, of course, thanks to you, the reader. Though you may never attend one of our presentations or hear one of our cassettes, may the "platform humor" of "Funnybone" give you a laugh, a break in the day or relaxation. May it help you expand your sense of humor into a priceless medium for persuasion, communication, and understanding.

When you have a minute, drop us a line, share a poem, a new quip or story. We'll trade you some thoughts for **any** letter you care to write us.

Sincerely,

Herb True

TEAM Int'l. Inc.
1717 E. Colfax Avenue
So. Bend, IN 46617
Phone: (219) 234-2340

P.S. For information about our cassettes, records and 8 track tapes on Humor, Motivation, Selling, Communications, or Leadership, write to me at the above address.

V

AGE

*The secret of staying young — is to
live honestly, eat slowly, sleep sufficiently,
work industriously, worship faithfully,
and then lie about your age.*

* * *

"You're still young if the morning after the night
before still makes the night before worth the morning
after."

* * *

On her 30th birthday a wife turned to her husband and said, "Will you love me when I grow old?"
He said, "Of course," then hesitated, "You aren't
going to look like your mother are you?"

* * *

Age does the same thing to people as it does to
wine — It sours the bad and improves the good.

1

My uncle lived to be 100, and he owes it to mushrooms. He never ate them.

* * *

The middle years. One man describes them as that quiet, peaceful, serene period between completing the children's college education and starting to help with the first grandchildren. "The middle years" he says "usually last from three to five months."

* * *

Maturity is the ability to do a job whether you are supervised or not, finish the job once it is started, carry money without spending it and the ability to bear an injustice without wanting to get even.

* * *

"Is it true that life begins at 40?"
"Begins to what?"

* * *

Old Mr. Got Rocks, fairly spry for his age, felt it necessary to resist the advances of an impoverished but eager widow of 32. "Mother and father are against it," he said gravely to her. "You are not going to tell me your mother and father are still alive?" "I am referring to Mother Nature and Father Time."

* * *

Remember when Sex Education was learning to kiss without bumping noses?

2

Remember when kids used to pick up extra money cleaning sidewalks? Now you hand them a snow shovel and they want to know where the plug is.

* * *

A woman who's going to celebrate her 80th birthday: When asked what she'd like for her birthday, she replied, "Just give me a kiss dear. That's one thing I won't have to dust."

* * *

A couple of elderly gents discussing longevity trade secrets — one being 85, the other exactly 100. Young feller: "How did YOU live to be a hundred?" Replied the elder, "Well, first you get to be 99 then you be careful as hell for a year."

* * *

Gentleman was asked: "How are you doing?" "Well," he said, "I'm drinking a fifth of whiskey a day, smoking a package of cigarettes and four cigars a day and have never felt better in my life." "You'd better watch out — all that high living might kill you." "Well, something better start killing me pretty soon. I'm 85 years old now."

* * *

Age doesn't really matter unless you are a cheese.

* * *

Middle age is when you know all the answers but nobody ever asks you the questions.

I have a neighbor who's 80 years old. His favorite comedy team is Masters and Johnson.

* * *

Student nurse had to give the elderly patient a shot. She asked which hip he wanted it in. He asked if he really had a choice. She said, "Yes." Looked her straight in the eye and said, "YOURS."

* * *

"The trip from wisdom to senility is very short. The tragic part of it is that the traveler himself usually is the last to know he's arrived."

* * *

He is at the age where being on speed means drinking Prune Juice.

* * *

"Tell me, Jasper." asked one of the old farmers in the country store, "Why do you treat that fellow with such respect?"

"Well Zeb," replied the owner, "It's because he's one of our early settlers."

"Can't be, Jasper. That young fellow isn't more than twenty-five years old."

"Not that kind of settler, Zeb. I mean he pays his bills on the first of every month."

* * *

Getting old is merely a matter of feeling your corns more than your oats.

"If America and her free institutions
are to prevail,
you have to serve MORE than your bosses;
deserve MORE than your paycheck;
and pay MORE than your taxes."

* * *

Let me ask you a question. When you hear them
talking about $89,000 in cash, $350,000 in cash,
$1,000,000 in cash; don't you feel a little silly
calling them cheap politicians?

* * *

"Well, I predict he'll go a long way in politics."
"Why do you say that?"
"He's mastered the three P's."
"Three P's?"
"Promises, promises, promises."

5

The future is so uncertain that for the first time in history, babies are being born with fingers crossed.

* * *

Question: I want to sign something that will live forever.
Answer: Sign a mortgage!

* * *

Americans are living in the lap of luxury. Sure hope we're not on our last lap.

* * *

April is the month that tells us — not only is Washington's face on our money, but Washington's hands are on it as well! It's a crazy world we live in. The strong take it away from the weak; the clever take it away from the strong; and the government takes it away from everybody!

* * *

My accountant had a clever idea. He told me to send in my estimated tax without signing it.
They want me to guess how much I'm going to earn, so, let them guess who sent it in.

* * *

Two Indians took keen interest in watching a lighthouse being built. After many months when it was finished, they stood staring at it when a thick fog began to roll in. "Ugh," said one, "Light shine, bell ring, horn blow, but fog comes in all the same."

6

Have you noticed how everybody's trying to cut corners? I just bought a suit with two pair of pants — but only one zipper.

* * *

In Indiana you can't vote if you're illiterate; but — you can get elected.

* * *

You'll have no trouble with crime, if you follow four simple suggestions:
1. Your door should be steel backed.
2. Your door should have a hidden peep-hole.
3. Your door should have a heavy duty, pick-proof lock.
4. Your door should be moved to Bangor, Maine.

* * *

Our enemies say the American flag looks like a peppermint stick. Maybe so, but it ain't never been licked.

* * *

Trouble with political jokes is that they often get elected to office.

* * *

As President, Herbert Hoover turned back all his salary to the Government. In those days, it was quite an event. Today, we all return our salaries to the government and nobody ever thinks much about it.

The world is run by those who are willing to sit until the end of meetings.

* * *

A man walked into the tax collector's office with his nose bandaged. The collector asked, "Had an accident on your nose?" "No," the fellow replied, "I've been paying through it for so long it gave way under the strain."

* * *

It's hard to believe that this country was founded partly to avoid taxes.

* * *

People say the dollar doesn't go for. It goes to India, Vietnam, Formosa, Pakistan, South America, and the Phillipines.

* * *

Am I wrong? I thought we had a deal with the post office. We were going to show a little code and they were going to show a little zip!

* * *

Detroit has finally come up with a pollution free car. It'll have tighter closing windows.

* * *

Inflation hasn't ruined everything. A dime can still be used as a screwdriver.

With our modern technology, we have now developed a 25 cent can of pop, which when discarded, lasts forever, AND a $4,000 car that, if taken good care of, will rust out in two years.

* * *

Youngster to old-timer: "Do you think it will rain soon?"

Old-timer: "When God was runnin' our country I could always predict the weather. Now that the Republicans is runnin' it, nobody can predict nothin."

* * *

Now, there's this folksinger who plays an Early American Electric Guitar. Comes fully equipped with a kite and key.

* * *

The reason newborn American babies cry is that they arrive with nothing to eat, nothing to wear, and owe the government about $4,000.

* * *

Pre-primary panel candidate took cheap shot at his opponent. "He is 43 years old, the son of a rich man and never worked a day in his life." After the panel, an old fellow walked up to the rich man and asked, "You the feller who's never worked a day in his life?" Wealthy man admitted he was. "Wal, let me tell you something, sonny," said the old man, "You ain't missed nuthin'."

Fellow wrote on a package he was about to mail: "Mailman — this is fragile, so please throw it underhand."

* * *

Tourist engaged an old Vermont farmer in conversation. "Tell me, old-timer, where did all these rocks come from?"

"Well son, I figure a glacier brought them."

"Oh," replied the tourist, "where's that glacier now?"

"Went back for more rocks, I reckon."

* * *

A presidential hopeful is so hungry for publicity that he carries a card in his wallet saying. "I am a candidate. In case of an accident, call a press conference."

* * *

AMERICA — *"Here lies the only civilization which perished at the peak of its potential power with its power misused. Here lies a decent people who wanted love, not an empire, and got neither; an earnest people who tried to trade power for popularity and lost both. Here lies a nation of advertisers who learned how to change consumer tastes in cigarettes but were themselves manipulated on all issues that really mattered to their salvation and survival. Here died a sort of Lancelot in the court of nations who granting all his flaws was still the noblest knight of all."*

10

CITIES and STATES

*I grew up in a home town where
all the families were big, poor and honest!
No one ever locked their doors.
There wasn't anything to steal but the kids.*

* * *

Did you hear about the Texan that was so rich he bought a boy for his dog! And still another rich Texan who doesn't even know he has a daughter in college.

* * *

There was a town, so small, that when they had an election they had to hire people to come in and vote.

* * *

What a crazy world this is! New York wants to get rid of their pigeons and Vegas is looking for more.

The California Freeway was the scene of a freak accident. Three freaks in a camper crashed into two freaks in a van.

* * *

"I nearly ran over a pedestrian a few minutes ago — and, I think he was from Miami."

"How did you know that?"

"Well, when he reached the sidewalk, I heard him say something about the sun and the beach."

* * *

I heard of a town, so small, that it was only open three days a week. Only had one yellow page in the telephone book, and the all night diner closed at 2:30 in the afternoon.

* * *

"The weather here in Florida is wonderful," said the elderly lady. "How do you tell summer from winter?"

Hotel clerk: "Well, in the winter we get Cadillacs, Lincolns, and stuffed shirts. In the summer we get Fords, Chevrolets and stuffed shorts."

* * *

New York tourist traveling through Texas panhandle, got into a conversation with an old settler and his son at a filling station. "Looks as though we might have rain," said the tourist.

"Well, I hope so — not so much for myself — but for my boy here. I've seen it rain!"

Woman was inching through the traffic in downtown Chicago one morning. She struck up a conversation with the man in the adjacent car. Noting that the time was 9:30 she remarked, "Well, I'm glad I wasn't in that 8:30 traffic." "I hate to tell you this, lady, but this IS the 8:30 traffic."

* * *

"Did you give your wife the money you won at the tables?"

"Sure thing, I told her to buy some decent clothes and she said, "I've worn decent clothes all of my life, now I'm going to dress like the other women."

* * *

Just got back from Vegas. Went there for a change and a rest. The slot machines got the change and the crap tables got the rest.

* * *

A guy went broke at the tables in Vegas. He met a friend and borrowed $20. Then borrowed $50 from him, which he blew. Hit him once more and got $100 with the advice: "Take this and get a bus and go home."

But — the fellow couldn't resist playing at the crap table again, only to lose the $100. He went into the men's room and told the attendant what had happened. The attendant advised: "There is only one thing to do, tap your friend once more." "Oh, no, I won't do that. That guy's bad luck!"

A tourist in Florida was admiring an Indian necklace made from alligator teeth. The storekeeper said it was more valuable than pearls. When the tourist wanted to know why, he said, "Lady, anyone can open an oyster."

* * *

"The trouble with Vegas is it gets so monotonous watching those beautiful girls dancing around on stage, and then wasting time drinking martinis and gambling . . and let me tell you something else my wife said the other day . . . "

* * *

I had a weird experience in Frisco. Opened a dresser drawer in the hotel and found Tony Bennett's heart.

* * *

"Listen! When I arrived in Detroit, I didn't have a cent. I not only didn't have any money in my pockets, I didn't have any pockets."
"How did that happen?"
"I was born in Detroit."

* * *

One way of doubling your money in the casino is to fold it and put it in your pocket.

* * *

Overheard on a plane landing in Nevada: "Just what are the grounds for divorce in this state?" — "Are you married?" — "Yes." — "Then you have grounds."

Communications

*Advantage to having an unlisted phone number —
If you get an obscene phone call,
at least you know it's from a friend.*

* * *

The downcast man said to his friend, "My wife doesn't understand me, does yours?"

The friend replied, "I don't know. I've never heard her mention you."

* * *

During a period of heavy flooding in Albany, the citizens were to get shots from the medical people to prevent typhoid. The residents were to get the shots according to voting precinct. One woman, after her identification to the medical officer, was told: "Lady, you'll have to get your shot in your precinct." "How come?" she complained. "All the others are getting them in their arms."

"We'll have to buy Junior an encyclopedia."

"What for?"

"He starts to school next week."

"Why can't he WALK to school like I did when I was a kid?"

* * *

A very deaf old gentleman decided that a hearing aid was much too expensive, so he got an ordinary piece of wire and wrapped it around his ear.

"Do you hear better now with that wire around your ear?" asked a friend.

"No, but everybody talks louder."

* * *

Telephone operator asked long distance caller:

"Do you have an area code?"

"No," came the sniffling reply. "It's a bad case of hay fever."

* * *

Woman went into small post office and asked for a dollar's worth of stamps. "What denomination?" asked the clerk. "Well, I didn't know it would ever come to this, but if the nosey Government people have to know, I'm a Baptist."

* * *

"Do you mind if I try that dress on in the window?" asked the customer.

"Not at all madam," replied the clerk, "but wouldn't you rather use the dressing room?"

Last time I went to the doctor, I saw the sign on his door. It said: "10 to 1". So, I went back home. I want better odds than that.

* * *

Banker's houseboat was sinking off Florida coast. He radioed for help. Coast Guard picked up his SOS and radioed back: "We are on the way . . . what is your position? . . . we repeat . . . what is your position?" "I'm Executive Vice-President of First National Bank, and please hurry."

* * *

I asked a lady on the program committee if it would be okay to send her a brochure. "No, I'm a member of women's lib and I don't wear them anymore."

* * *

Lobbyist who was opposing ANY large appropriation, approached a legislator who boasted of his self-education. "Do you realize," asked the lobbyist, gravely, "that up at the state college, men and women students have to use the same curriculum?"

Legislator looked startled.

"And that boys and girls often matriculate together?"

"No!" exclaimed the lawmaker.

The lobbyist came close and whispered, "And a young lady student can be forced at any time to show a male professor her thesis . . ."

The legislator shrank back in horror: "I won't vote 'em a damned cent!"

17

Handsome young executive was making himself useful by asking the passengers for their floors and pushing the elevator buttons for them. A pretty secretary got on at the second floor and he asked: "Do you get off at five?" Smiling she answered: "No, but I can meet you at 5:30."

* * *

One fellow said he's sorry he put a phone in his car. Running to the garage every time it rings is a nuisance.

* * *

Words are so important! I was telling our 6 year old —. "When you talk to the neighbors, just say that your aunt likes to crochet. Don't call her the happy hooker."

* * *

Two men from the Ozarks decided to visit a museum. In the Egyptian wing they stood staring at a mummy case bearing the inscription 1256 B.C.
"What do you make of them numbers, Zeke?"
"Well," replied the mountaineer, "Can't rightly say, lessen it's the license number of the car that killed him."

* * *

I called my landlord and said my apartment had terrible acoustics, and he wrote back and said that he caught them all long before I moved in.

18

Lad: "I want to marry your daughter."
Dad: "Have you seen my wife yet?"
Lad: "Yes, I have, but I prefer your daughter."

* * *

A man and his Indian guide were camping in the Everglades. In the middle of the night, the man woke up yelling that an alligator had bitten off his foot.

"Which one?" asked his guide.

"How should I know." the man moaned. "They all look alike to me."

* * *

Mortified lady motorist was called before a village Justice of the Peace by motorcycle cop who announced: "Judging by the way this here woman handles a car in traffic, I don't think she can see very well."

Justice didn't look too surprised. "We'll just give her the little old eye-test." he said. "Lady, please read the third line on that chart on the wall."

Without hesitation the lady spelled out: "Y – M – P – J – C."

"Perfect," approved the Justice, "Now read the line at the very bottom."

"I would like to purchase," read the lady, "some tickets for the Policemen's pageant and field day."

"Better still," boomed the Justice. "how many?"

The Sunday school teacher asked her pupils if they understood the meaning of "False doctrine."

"Yes," said a little boy. "False doctrine is when the doctor gives you the wrong kind of medicine."

* * *

"Miss Jones! Do you retire a loan?"
"No sir! I sleep with my aunt."

* * *

Old mountain man watching storekeeper unwrap brightly colored men's pajamas.

"What's that?"
"Pajamas."
"What are they for?"
"You wear them at night. Would you like to buy a pair?"
"Nope! Don't go no place at night except to bed."

* * *

He wanted to do a little remodeling and called in a housepainter for an estimate. Painter said he'd take the job for seven hundred dollars.

"Seven hundred dollars!" cried the outraged homeowner. "Why, I wouldn't pay Van Gogh that much."

"Oh, yeah?" replied the painter. "If he does the job for any less, he'll have to cross a picket line first."

20

OPPORTUNITIES GALORE
WHEN CREATIVITY IS KING

MODIFY —
Color, shape, sound, odor, motion, meaning

REARRANGE —
Sequence, pace, components, schedule, pattern

OBVIOUS — Imitate, transfer, suggestive, copy

REVERSE —
Backward, upside down, direct, opposite

MAGNIFY —
Units, action, price, higher, longer, thicker

REDUCE —
Miniature, omit, shorten, split, condense

SUBSTITUTE —
Ingredients, power, process, approach

ADAPT — Outright, related, reborn, new uses

BASIC WANTS —
Personalize, emulate, senses, anticipated

COMBINE —
Blends, units, assortments, ensembles, ideas

Secretary comfortable on the bosses lap when he spied, through the window of his office partition, his wife approaching. As she entered the door, he began to dictate rapidly. "Take this letter to the A.B.C. Furniture Co. — Shortages or no shortages, how long do you think I can run my office with only one chair?"

* * *

There was a man who got tired of receiving "junk mail."

So, he returned every letter in that category to the Post Office, writing the word "Deceased" across the envelope. Now his wife gets letters from tombstone companies.

* * *

Grandma's formula for peaceful baby sitting: Put molasses on his fingers and then give him a feather to play with!

* * *

Personnel director of airplane factory received a questionnaire which asked. "How many employees do you have broken down by sex?" Director wrote back. "Liquor is more of a problem with us."

* * *

Management offered a $25 cash bonus to employees whose suggestions would save the company money. First winner — the man who suggested lowering the bonus to $10.

Have you ever heard of enthusiastic stew? They call it enthusiastic stew because the cook puts everything he has into it.

* * *

Fellow wrote in to company, "I'm interested in your product but don't send any salesman." Two days later, salesman appears.

Fellow says. "I thought I said no salesman?"

"Sir, I'm the closest thing to 'no salesman' that we have."

* * *

If you don't use your arm for three months, it becomes stiff and solid. What about your mind?

* * *

Guy goes to psychologist and says: "Can't go to sleep at nite. Little animals are running up and down my bed. What should I do?"

Psychologist: "For $50 I will cure it."

Patient: "That crazy I am not. I will find something else."

Six months later, psychologist meets him again and says, "How is your problem?"

Patient: "I solved it."

Psychologist: "How, another psychologist?"

Patient: "No, I went to my brother."

Psychologist: "Is he a psychologist?"

Patient: "No, he is a carpenter."

Psychologist: "What did he do?"

Patient: "He cut off the legs of the bed."

Made a long distance call and when I was through the operator said. "That will be $14.55." I said, $14.55? I told you to reverse the charges." "All right! That'll be $55.41.

* * *

"Mommy," said little Johnny, "can I have a quarter for the man outside who is crying?"

"Certainly, dear," said his mother, "but what is he crying about?"

"Well," admitted Johnny, "he's crying, 'Ice cream, ice cream, twenty-five cents for ice cream'."

* * *

Question: What's the difference between this British bicycle and this American one?
Answer: Sir, the British bike is made in England.

* * *

Father of lovely 18 year old girl found out that his daughter had hitchhiked alone from Seattle to San Diego.

"You could have been molested, assaulted, or raped," he said.

"I was perfectly safe," she said, "Everytime a lone man picked me up I always told him I was going to San Diego because that city had the best VD clinic on the West Coast."

* * *

A lady down the block says nearly everybody is a genius up to the age of 10.

definitions

"A gentlemen's agreement is one
that neither party wants to put in writing."

* * *

Ad-libber: A comic who spends hours memorizing
spontaneous jokes.

* * *

Dirty old man: "One with 4 teenagers and
one bathroom."

* * *

A real executive is a man who can hand back
a letter for a third retyping to a red-headed steno-
grapher.

* * *

Egomaniac: A person who doesn't go around talking about other people.

Jury: 12 men or women chosen to decide who has the better lawyer.

* * *

Instant: The length of time it takes a super-market cash register to reach $10.

* * *

Minute Man: One who can make it to the refrigerator and back while the commercial is on.

* * *

An experienced after-dinner speaker was asked what he considered to be a perfect audience.

"Oh, to me," he said, "the perfect audience is one that is well educated, highly intellegent — and just a little bit drunk."

* * *

Confusion: A fire drill during phys. ed. shower.

* * *

Opera: Where a guy gets stabbed in the back but instead of bleeding — he sings.

* * *

College bred: A 4 year loaf made with father's dough.

* * *

Success: When you have your name in everything but the telephone directory.

Daffynition of critics: "People who go places and boo things."

* * *

Naturalist: A guy who throws sevens.

* * *

Faith: Something you believe in when you don't have anything to believe in.

* * *

"A summer camp is where parents spend $1,000 so their daughter can learn to make a 50 cent potholder."

* * *

A coach is the guy who is always happy to lay down YOUR life for HIS job.

* * *

An athiest is a man who has no invisible means of support.

* * *

Public opinion is what folks THINK folks THINK.

* * *

A high school boy was doing his homework in social science. He said to his father, "What is it they call a person who brings you into contact with the world and things?"

"A bartender, son," his father said.

Television: Summer Stock in an iron lung.

* * *

"Thank you! You're really doing a fine job. A fine job. I just hope you never look up the word 'fine' in the dictionary. It means 'very small'."

* * *

You know a man is a celebrity when the newspapers start quoting him on subjects he knows nothing about.

* * *

Arthritis: Twinges in the hinges.

* * *

Asked to define heredity, a small girl wrote: "Heredity means that if your parents didn't have any children, you won't have any either."

* * *

Income Tax: The annual guaranteed rage.

* * *

The professor of political science asked his class, "Can any one of you give me a clear, concise, easy to understand definition of a politician?"
"Yes, sir, I can," said a young fellow, "Just tell me whether you mean a Republican or a Democrat."

* * *

A theory is a hunch with a college education.

EDUCATION

"The test of a first rate intelligence
is the ability to hold
two opposing ideas in mind at the same time
and still retain the ability to function."
For example, the ability to see things as hopeless
and yet to be determined to make them otherwise.
Gun Control — Abortion — Tankers — Etc.

* * *

Know a lady who said she would rather starve than
teach school — Now she is doing both!

* * *

Two chorus girls were shopping together one
day. "I just don't know what to get Jean for her
birthday," said the first one.

"Why don't you get her a book?" suggested
the other.

"No," said the first, "she's got a book."

A boy asked his father, "What is college-bred, dad?"
His father, with another son at the University, said,
"College bread is made from the flower of youth
and the dough of old age."

* * *

The oldtimer remembers when the Board of
Education was a hair brush.

* * *

Principal to visitor: "Don't get upset if you hear the
girls discussing the pill. They're talking about me."

* * *

A man and his little son are riding on a bus.
The boy, his nose pressed against the window, keeps
asking his father questions:
"What's on that truck, daddy?"
"I dunno," mumbles the father immersed in
his paper.
"Where does the rain come from?"
"Don't bother me."
"What does that sign say?"
"Quit pestering me."
A passenger behind them taps the father on
the shoulder, "Curious little boy you've got there!"
"Sure," says the father. "How else will he
learn?"

* * *

Teaching school is like having a baby. They both
take 9 months and the last day is the worst.

"What is your son taking in college?"
"All I've got."

* * *

"Has your boy's education been of value?"
"Yup! It cured his ma of bragging about him."

* * *

Teacher took the first grade class on a field trip to a museum of natural history.

That night when the first grader's father came home he asked what he'd done in school that day.

"Well, we went to a dead circus."

* * *

My son refuses to study history anymore. He claims they make it faster than he can learn it.

* * *

"How long are you planning to teach school?" dean asked pretty young thing as he handed her her teaching certificate.

"From here to maternity," she replied with a smile.

* * *

Rejected by the college of his choice, the banker's son angrily accosted his father. "If you really cared for me, you would have pulled some wires." "I know. The TV, the Hi-Fi, and the telephone would have done for a start."

The father was telling the candidate about his family. "Nine boys," he said, "and all Democrats, except John. He learned to read."

* * *

First day back to classes after long absence: Grade school teacher said, "It was like trying to hold 35 corks under water at the same time."

* * *

My kid isn't too bright. I bought him an electric blanket and he tried to play it.

* * *

Student attended only first lecture, returned for final exam and received grade of 90. Puzzled prof called in student to ask about absence. Student immediately took the offensive. "I know you called me in here about the grade of 90. I'd have done better but I attended one lecture and that really confused me."

* * *

"How do you spell Mississippi?"
"River or State?"

* * *

Today we live by the great lessons given the world by the early sages. Socrates taught us democracy. Aristotle taught us logic. Caesar taught us military tactics and even crazy Emperor Nero, who set Rome on fire, taught us something. Slum clearance!

HEALTH

"If the Lord meant us to be
on our toes all the time,
He wouldn't have given us
so much to sit down with."

* * *

He is so anemic, when a mosquito lands
on him, all it gets is practice.

* * *

Sammy Davis is driving 90 miles an hour in Vegas.
They lock him up for speeding and the judge says,
"Are you crazy? 90 miles an hour!" Sammy says,
"What do you want? I only got one eye. Do you
want me to watch the road or the speedometer?"

* * *

According to my weight and height I'm
not as old as I should be!

Just heard about a man that was run over by a steam roller. He 's in Memorial Hospital in Rooms 102 to 107.

* * *

Amazing things can be done with only simple tools. For example: A man can build a big bay window with a knife and fork alone.

* * *

It's quite a shock getting your first pair of bifocals. You look down and you have the same problem as Raquel Welch. You can't see your feet.

* * *

I'm in perfect health. In fact, there's only one thing harder than my muscles. My arteries.

* * *

"You've got to give up smoking, " the doctor said.

"I don't smoke," said the patient.

"Well, then, you've got to give up coffee," the doctor insisted.

"Never drink it," the patient told him.

"Whiskey," the doctor said. "You've got to give up whiskey."

"But," said the man, "I don't drink whiskey either."

"What do you do?" the doctor shouted at him. "If you don't have anything to give up, how do you expect me to be able to treat you?"

A Congressman was speaking on the floor of the House, when one of his colleagues shouted, "You are out of order."

The Congressman stopped his speech and said, "Just how am I out of order?"

"How should I know?" shouted the other Congressman. "Why don't you go see a veterinarian?"

* * *

Two firemen risked their lives to save a drunk from a hotel fire. His bed was in flames when they found him, and one of the firemen demanded, "Don't you know better than to smoke in bed? You could have burned up the whole hotel." The drunk looked sheepish and replied, "Honest, mister, I wasn't smoking in bed. The bed was on fire when I got in."

* * *

A newspaper reporter was interviewing a man on his 99th birthday. As he was shaking hands to leave, he said, "I hope I can come back next year and see you on your 100th birthday."

"I don't see why you can't," said the old man, "you look healthy enough."

* * *

"Henry, you are drunk," said his wife as they waited for the parking lot attendant to bring them their car. "Don't you know why they say, "Don't drink when you drive?"

"I sure do," said Henry. "You might hit a bump and spill some."

35

If medical science has made so much progress, how come I feel so much worse than I did 20 years ago?

* * *

Wife to hungover husband: "What do you mean, you have nothing to live for? The house is mortgaged, the car isn't paid for, you still owe on the TV and you've got a dilly of a loan with HFC."

* * *

Two drunks accidentally wandered into an amusement park and boarded a roller coaster. The ride was fast and furious, but it didn't seem to make much of an impression. As they were getting off, one drunk was heard to say, "You know, we may have made good time, but I have a feeling we took the wrong bus."

* * *

A man visited his optometrist to have his glasses checked. "They just aren't strong enough," he told the doctor. "Don't you have something stronger?"

"Yes," said the optometrist, "There is one lens that is stronger."

"Just one?" asked the man. "What comes after that?"

"After that," the doctor said, "you buy a dog."

* * *

You can become bald at 25 but you have to shave every day of your life.

36

IMPORTED HUMOR

*Do you realize that nine-tenths of the people
who live in the countries
that have three-fourths of the world's gas
ride on camels!*

* * *

Russian correspondent wired his office that
American automobiles are so inefficient they have
to be pushed along the highways by boat.

* * *

An irate Italian policeman was in the process
of arresting an unruly and very drunk American
tourist.

"It is my duty to inform you," said the cara-
biniere sternly, "that just as in your country, anything you say may be held against you."

"That's wonderful," said the drunken tourist.
"How about 'Sophia Loren'?"

37

"Say something sparkling in French."
"Bon Ami!"

* * *

What does U.S.S. stand for in the United States
Navy? — United States Ship.
What does H.M.S. stand for in the British Navy?
Her (His) Majesty's Ship.
What does A.M.B. stand for in the Italian Navy?
"Atsa My Boat!"

* * *

In South Bend "foreign affairs" is having a
girl friend in Chicago.

* * *

Famed Chinese diplomat attended gala recep-
tion in Washington in early part of day. Senate lady,
trying to make polite conversation asked. "Dr.
Wong, what 'nese' are you? Chinese, Japanese, or
Javanese?"

"Chinese," he replied, " and you madam? What
'kee' are you? Monkey, donkey or yankee."

* * *

Man vacationing in London sent in this observation: This is a very high-class town. Even the
poor people have British accents.

* * *

Hear about the ship sailing from Hong Kong with
a cargo of YoYo's. Sank in a storm 164 times.

LOVE & MARRIAGE

Your Love Is True If You:
   Think of him or her more than anyone else;
   Desire to be with him or her over anyone else;
   Make real efforts and go out of your way
      to try to please them;
   Make sacrifices for them without expecting
      reciprocal acts;
   Try almost superhuman ways to avoid
      alienating their friends;
   Feel an obligation and often explain and
      defend their actions;
   Have real pain when they are hurting or low;
   Have more generosity for everybody
      and everything when you're around them;
   Plan not only your present but your future
      with them in mind.

* * *

   Love is like a mushroom! It's difficult to tell
whether it's the real thing until it's too late.

Marriage teaches you loyalty, tolerance, understanding, perserverance, and a lot of other things you wouldn't need if you had stayed single.

* * *

A hopeful young lady visited a computer dating service and listed her requirements: She wanted someone who liked people, was small, preferred formal attire and enjoyed water sports. The computer followed her wishes to the letter. It sent her a penguin.

* * *

Doctor: "You won't live a week if you don't stop running around with women."
Patient: "Oh, there is nothing wrong with me. I'm in great shape."
Doctor: "Yeah, I know, but one of those women is my wife."

* * *

Young housewife presented her husband's paycheck for payment and the teller explained that it had to be endorsed first. She looked thoughtful and then wrote on the back of the check . . . "My husband is a wonderful man."

* * *

There was an unusual auction at our church yesterday. All the parishioners were asked to bring something to auction off that they didn't have use for — and forty women brought their husbands.

Some people are funny! I knew of a man who hadn't kissed his wife for 10 years, but he went and shot the fellow who did.

* * *

Talk about being generous. Why, I knew a guy who was so generous with his girl friend that he finally had to marry her for his money.

* * *

Wife to surly looking husband who is shaving: "What would you like thrown into your cage for breakfast this morning?"

* * *

"If I had to do it again, I'd marry a Japanese girl. They're pretty, graceful, obedient — and they are attentive," a wishful male dreamed aloud.

"And besides, your mother-in-law would be in Tokyo," his friend concluded.

* * *

"What's worse than being a bachelor? — Being a bachelor's son!"

* * *

"This is your 4th marriage," said an acquaintance to the divorcee, "first to a banker, then to an actor, then to a minister, and now to an undertaker. Why did you marry men in these particular jobs?"

"Oh, that's easy. One for the money, two for the show, three to make ready, and four to go."

He was in love with a twin. "Did you ever kiss the other by mistake?"

"Are you kidding? Her brother has a beard."

* * *

There is nothing wrong with marriage. It's all that living together afterwards that causes the trouble.

* * *

Our neighbor's wife divorced him because he gave her a fur wrap. He hit her right in the mouth with the cat!

* * *

For 30 years a guy secretly met a gal each Wednesday without his wife ever finding out. His wife passed away and he married his Wednesday gal. Now he doesn't know what to do on Wednesdays.

* * *

They were married for twenty-five years and had their biggest argument on the day of their silver anniversary. "If it weren't for my money, that TV set wouldn't be here. If it weren't for my money, the very chair you're sitting on wouldn't be here!"

"Are you kidding?" he interrupted, "if it weren't for your money — I wouldn't be here!"

* * *

When a girl says she never drinks anything stronger than pop, maybe you'd better check on what pop drinks.

42

Mother to small daughter: "All right, I'll tell you about sex. It leads to housework."

* * *

"When did you first know that you loved me?"
"When I began to get mad at people who said you were brainless and homely."

* * *

Fellow ran into the fire engine house and very excitedly shouted: "I'm sorry to bother you, but my wife has disappeared again."
"That's too bad, but why tell us? Why not notify the police?"
"Well, I'll tell you. I told the police the last time she disappeared and they went and found her."

* * *

Last night my wife asked me if I thought the excitement had gone out of our marriage. I told her we'd discuss it during the commercial!

* * *

Husband to wife: "What do you say we take the money we have saved toward a new car and go out and blow it on a movie?"

* * *

Husband: "For twenty years my wife and I were ecstatically happy."
Friend: "Then what happened?"
Husband: "We met!"

In marriage no wife ever gets what she expected and no husband expects what he gets.

* * *

Annoyed wife to husband: "Can't you say that we've been married 25 years instead of a quarter of a century?"

* * *

Arriving home unexpectedly, Henry found his wife in the arms of his best friend. "Well, I'm glad to finally have this out," exclaimed the friend. "I love your wife and want her for my own. Let's be gentlemen and settle this with a game of cards. Winner takes Emily, all right? Shall we play gin rummy?" "Sounds fine to me, but how about a penny a point just to make the game interesting?"

* * *

When asked how he had proposed to his wife he replied: "It was a beautiful night. The moon was full — and I was a little loaded myself!"

* * *

" All right," said the unhappy wife to husband, "I admit I like to spend money . . . but, name one other extravagance I have."

* * *

A fellow admitted he and his wife have little in common: "The last time we did anything together was getting married on the same day."

"Sir, I've just met this girl and even as I write this I tingle all over. A vibrant thrill is going thru me and my blood courses like fire thru my veins. Am I in love? . . ."

"Maybe! But first, push your writing desk back — your toe may be in the wall socket."

* * *

Husband: "I saw Tim Tolley downtown today and he didn't even speak to me. I guess he thinks I'm not his equal."

Wife: "Why, that stupid, brainless, conceited, good for nothing moron! You certainly "are" his equal!"

* * *

New bumper sticker: "Fight poverty — stay single!"

* * *

"You always hurt the one you love," said the porcupine.

* * *

Psychiatrists say that girls tend to marry men like their father . . . now we know why mothers cry at weddings.

* * *

A salesman's wife had been bugging him for a mink for months. He finally gave in and promised her one for her birthday but on one condition. She has to keep it's cage clean.

Only ideal marriage was that of Adam and Eve. He didn't have to hear about the men she could have married and she didn't have to hear about the way his mother cooked.

* * *

A pretty young lady in Ohio had a persistent but undesired suiter in New York. He pressed an ardent campaign for her hand through the mails, sending a special delivery letter twice a day for 63 days. On the 64th day, the campaign produced results. The girl ran off with the mailman!

* * *

"I prefer older men — someone I won't have to put through college."

* * *

Son: "Daddy, why is a man only allowed to have one wife?"
Dad: "Son, when you grow older you will understand the law protects those who are unable to protect themselves."

* * *

A little fellow approached the marriage license window at the county courthouse and stated that he would like to have a permit to marry. The attendant at the window asked, "Where's the bride-elect?" "There warn't no election," said the applicant, pointing to the dominant woman immediately behind him. "She done appointed herself."

* * *

MANAGEMENT AND BUSINESS

Half of the problems of the human race are due to the lack of business knowledge of what IS their business and what is NONE of their business.

* * *

"See here, Jones, I'm fed up with you getting your hair cut on company time."

"It GROWS on company time."

"It doesn't all grow on company time."

"I don't get it all cut off."

* * *

"Gee, Mr. Bangelstein, I hope you never get one of these new office machines. It says here in the paper that it will replace three women."

"You mean it will go to the washroom 18 times, make 107 personal phone calls, take 5 coffee breaks, take up office collections twice a week, and get pregnant in the busy season?"

Always give the good news first. Like the mechanic who said, "Your glove compartment and sun visor are in good condition. Now, about your transmission."

* * *

The owner of a shoe store was asked: "How's business?"

"Pretty good," he said. "I haven't had a customer all day."

"What's so good about that?" his friend asked.

"See that fellow over there?" the man said, pointing to the shoe store across the street. "Well, he hasn't had a customer in two days."

* * *

If auto makers expect to stop dirtying our environment, they will have to stop putting Mustangs and Pintos on the road.

* * *

An old farmer went into the hardware store and bought a dozen axe handles at $1.25 each. In a little while he came back and bought a dozen more at the same price. The clerk asked: "If you don't mind my asking, what are you doing with all the axe handles?"

"I'm selling 'em."

"What do you get for them?"

"I get a buck a piece."

"Well, you don't make any money that way."

"No, I don't. But I tell ya this, it shore beats farmin'."

48

Things aren't always what they seem to be. For instance, every morning downtown a little old man with a happy smile feeds 2,000 pigeons. Some think he is a bird lover. They are wrong. He is a drycleaner.

* * *

Did you ever stop to realize that if all the cars were painted red, we'd have a red-car-nation!

* * *

Corn is a peculiar commodity. In the Midwest it's measured by the foot, in the South by the fifth and on TV by the hour.

* * *

The tighter the money, the higher the interest! It's the same with women's slacks.

* * *

If the bank in Red Bank, New Jersey buys the bank in Long Branch, New Jersey, it will be called: The Long Branch branch of the Red Bank bank.

* * *

A guy called a plumber the other day to fix a couple of leaks. When the repairs were finished, the guy asked for the bill and the plumber told him he would mail it to him.

"Why not give it to me now?"

"Because," said the plumber, "I hate to see a grown man cry."

49

There was the polite bank robber who walked into the bank with pistol drawn and said: "Ladies and Gentlemen, those in favor of leaving these premises alive will kindly hold up their hands."

* * *

Did you hear about the auto mechanic who bought a hospital and he is making a fortune? You take your wife in for an operation and they give you a loaner.

* * *

Iron worker descended from skeleton of new skyscraper and a man who had been watching asked:
"How do you happen to go to work on a job like this?"
"I used to drive a school bus but my nerves gave out."

* * *

Doing business without advertising is like winking at a girl in the dark; you know what you're doing, but nobody else does.

* * *

The tourist was talking to the man who had just celebrated his ninetieth birthday. "And to what do you owe your great age?" he asked.
"Well, I'm not sure yet," the man said. "I'm still dickering with a couple of breakfast food companies."

50

A note from a creditor said: "We know you have this little obligation in the back of your mind, but won't you please move it up front?"

* * *

One out of every six bank directors in New York City is over the age of 70. The trick is to find the senile one when you want a loan.

* * *

"What's wrong with the computer?" the office manager asked.

"Someone dropped a rubber band in it and now it's making snap decisions."

* * *

"Is there any soup on the menu?"
"There was, but I wiped it off."

* * *

Secretary to Secretary: "We call him the office locomotive. All he does is run back and forth, smoke and whistle."

* * *

"My husband," explained Mrs. Brown, " is an efficiency expert for a large company."

"Imagine that," said Mrs. Jones, "but what does an efficiency expert do?"

Mrs. Brown gave the matter some thought. "Well, I'm not sure I can describe it exactly, but when I do it he calls it nagging."

One of life's big disappointments in discovering that the man who writes the advertisements for a bank is not the same guy who makes the loans.

* * *

A Collection Company uses this trick: It's supposedly a two page letter but when the recipient opens it, he finds that the first page of the letter is missing. At the top of the second page it reads, "Now you wouldn't want us to do that, would you?"

* * *

Auto manufacturer received the following call:
    "Was it your company that announced you recently put a car together in 17 minutes?"
    "Yes, sir, it was."
    "Well, then I'd just like to let you know that I am the owner of that car."

* * *

If you want to see the stock market charts hit new highs . . . hold them upside down.

* * *

Collection Agency reports success with the following dun: "If you don't pay what you owe, we'll tell your other creditors you did."

* * *

He went into business on a shoestring and trippled his investment. What gets me, is what is he going to do with three shoestrings?

52

NEW

NEW MODEL: A TV set that automatically dispenses a stiff drink just before the 6 o'clock news.

* * *

Newspapers: We are not certain whether people are getting worse or whether the papers are keeping us better informed.

* * *

Progress isn't always for the best. For example, smoke signals never got an Indian out of bed at 3 in the morning to answer a wrong number.

* * *

A service station attendant asked the customer if he wanted new lead free gas. "No," replied the customer emphatically, "I remember when they put lead into the gas and RAISED the price, now, I'll be darned if I'm going to pay extra for taking it out."

53

Look out the window while eating breakfast. You'll see a bird after a worm, a cat ready to pounce on the bird, and the dog is after the cat. This will give you a better understanding of today's news.

* * *

A newly graduated journalism student said to a seasoned editor, "I'd like some advice on how to run a newspaper."

"You've come to the wrong man," the editor said, "You should ask one of our subscribers."

* * *

With new laws prohibiting classified ads to differentiate between job openings for men and women . . you may have seen the following:

"Pregnant men or women wanted to model maternity wear."

"Men or women wanted to do razor blade commercials on TV. Must have heavy beard."

"Topless go-go dancers wanted. Must have good legs and no hair on chest."

* * *

Most readable want ad of the year: "Hundred year old brass bed, $100. Perfect for antique lover."

* * *

Lost and Found: Found, Lady's purse left in my car while parked. Owner can have same by paying for this ad. If she will explain to my wife just how her purse got into my car, then I will pay for ad.

I love to read those advice columns in the news--paper. Read one this morning. "Dear Gabby: What is the worst thing a wife can get on her 25th wedding anniversary?" Know what the answer was . . . "Morning sickness."

* * *

A woman whose husband disappeared, asked a girl at the newspaper classified desk, how much an ad would cost asking her man to return. She was informed that the standard charge was $1 an inch, so she quickly changed her mind. She thought the cost was too much since her husband was 6'4" tall.

* * *

Help Wanted: Auto Mechanic. Must look honest.

* * *

The following testimony was given in Police court where a stripper was being tried on charges of giving an indecent performance.

"Were you covered by anything at all during your performance?" the district attorney asked.

"I certainly was," the young woman replied.

"What, specifically?"

"The witness hesitated a moment, then said triumphantly, "Workers Compensation."

* * *

Wanted: A small cottage by a gentleman with a big bay window."

Ad: Wanted! Job in a dynamite factory, chemical plant or other highly inflammable or explosive area. Trying to quit smoking.

* * *

Lost: A thick pair of reading glasses. Finder please advertise in large print.

* * *

"Author, psychologist, wants secretary. College graduate who has majored in any subject except psychology."

* * *

Poland solves Energy Crisis! It is going to import 200 billion tons of sand from Saudi Arabia and drill for its own oil.

* * *

A newspaper reporter was interviewing the famous octogenarian. "If you had your life to live over," he asked, " do you think you'd make the same mistakes again?"

" Certainly," said the old man, "but I'd start a lot sooner."

* * *

A big city reporter asked a small town editor why people bought his newspaper since they already knew what had happened and what everybody in town had done that week. "They buy the paper because they want to see which ones got caught!"

56

AN OPTIMIST IS A PERSON WHO:
Is always talking about what a fool he used to be.

Starts putting on his shoes when the speaker says, "and now, in conclusion . . ."

Marries his secretary, thinking he'll continue to dictate to her.

Believes that the cleaners are shrinking his pants when he's really gaining weight.

Thinks his wife has given up, when she has given in.

Thinks the man she is about to marry is better than the one she just divorced.

* * *

Most human beings are incurable optimists! They believe they have a pretty good chance to win a lottery prize but scarcely the slightest chance of getting killed in a traffic accident.

An optimist is the one who thinks that taxes can't go any higher.

* * *

A pessimist is one who would complain about the noise if opportunity knocked.

* * *

An optimist can hand his car over to a parking lot attendant without looking back.

* * *

A pessimist is an individual who thinks all the good old days were in the past; an optimist thinks they're all in the future.

* * *

An optimist thinks this is the best of all possible worlds. The pessimist is afraid they are right.

* * *

A pessimist is one who can only see the hole in the doughnut.

* * *

An optimist is a man who thinks he can build a $30,000 house for $30,000.

* * *

A pessimist remembers that the lily belongs to the onion family, while an optimist remembers that the onion belongs to the lily family.

PROFESSIONS

Walking helps, my doctor says,
both physical and mental.
But every time I see him . . .
he's in his Continental

* * *

With acupuncture becoming so popular, there may soon be a Mao Clinic.

* * *

Practical Nurse: She fell in love with a rich patient.

* * *

Lawyers: The only people I know who can write a 10,000 word document and call it a brief.

* * *

"Mrs. Jones, your check came back."
"I know Doctor. So did my arthritis."

One of the greatest criminal lawyers in the nation recently got an urgent telephone call from one of his clients. Said the client to the lawyer: "I'm in prison and they've shaved my head, transferred me to Death-Row, cut a slit in my trousers; what should I do?"

Said the lawyer: "Don't sit down!"

* * *

"I've brought you a Red Cross nurse," said the doctor.

"Take her back," yelled the patient, " and get me a blond, cheerful one."

* * *

Once upon a time, the fence between Heaven and Hell broke down. St. Peter appeared at the broken section and called out to the devil: "Hey Satan, since all the engineers are over in your place, how about getting them to fix this fence?" "Sorry," replied Satan, " My men are all too busy to go about fixing measly fences." "Well, then," replied St. Peter,"I'll have to sue you if you don't." "Oh yeah," countered the devil, " and where are you going to get a lawyer?"

* * *

I had an ulcer flareup the other day. Went to the doctor for an examination and he said: "The only thing I'm going to prescribe for you is exercise . . . a little skipping. Like skip smoking, skip drinking, skip rich foods . . ."

Specialist: A doctor with a smaller practice but a larger yacht.

* * *

Judge: "What possible excuse can you give for acquitting this man?"
Jury Foreman: "Insanity, Your Honor."
Judge: "All twelve of you?"

* * *

On the welcome mat outside the obstetrician's office. "This is where you come when you're thru playing games."

* * *

Two lawyers were bosom friends. Much to the amazement of one of them, the other became a Sunday School teacher.

"Why," he protested, "I'll bet you don't even know the Lord's Prayer."

"Everybody knows that. It's 'Now I lay me down to sleep'."

"You win," said the other admiringly. "I didn't know you knew so much about the Bible.

* * *

They say medical science is improving all the time, but I've never read of a cemetery going bankrupt.

* * *

He was one of those relaxed lawyers. He passed the bar ten years ago and he hasn't passed one since.

Lady doctor married psychiatrist. They get along fine. She makes him sick and he drives her nuts.

* * *

"Boy, what a lawyer."
"This guy was sentenced to the electric chair and . . ."
"What did the lawyer do for him?"
"He got the voltage reduced."

* * *

A slander action had been fought bitterly thru the courts for several weary days. Finally, the judge got down to the essentials and asked the defense what he had said.

"Sir, I merely observed that he was a sculpture who ought to wash more often."

"That seems innocuous enough," said the judge. "But what were your exact words?"

"I said he was a dirty chiseler."

* * *

A fellow we know confides that his lawyer is reopening a case they lost, on the grounds of new evidence. "He found out I have another $500 left."

* * *

A man I know was going to have an operation. The doctor told him it would cost $200 down and $50 a month for the next 18 months. "Sounds like buying a small car." "How did you guess?" asked the doctor in surprise.

On visiting a critically ill lawyer in the hospital, a friend found him propped up in bed frantically leafing thru the Bible. "What are you doing," he questioned. "Looking for loopholes," he replied.

* * *

Finnegan never ran away from a fight but when it came to having dental work done, he cried like a baby. The dentist realizing this said, "Pat, here's a tot of whiskey to get up your courage. Got the courage now?" — "NO," replied Pat. The dentist gave him three more and added one more for good measure. "How do you feel now?" he asked. "I'd like to see the idiot who'd dare to touch me teeth now," spouted Pat.

* * *

"I don't think I've ever seen a $200 bill."
"Really? I have one. I'll show it to you."
"You have a $200 bill?"
"Of course, it's from my dentist."

* * *

A fireman risked his life to save a beautiful young girl. As he carried her half-naked body from the burning building she whispered, "You're so brave. It must have taken a great deal of courage to rescue me."

"It sure did," admitted the noble fireman. "First I had to fight three other guys who wanted to save you."

He works on a contingency basis. That's an old gold mining term meaning — he gets the gold and you get the shaft.

* * *

The doctor gave his patient six months to live. The patient couldn't pay his bill so the doctor gave him another 6 months.

* * *

Woman went to a doctor and said, "I got a terrible problem with my husband. He fills the tub half full of water and gets in with waders and fishing pole and then fishes in the lavatory."
"Have you seen a psychiatrist?" he inquires.
"No, I've been too busy cleaning the fish."

* * *

The doctor promised to have me on my feet within a month and he wasn't kidding. I had to sell my car to pay his bill.

* * *

A nurse reports that she overheard a doctor telling a somewhat hypochondriacal patient, "Just drink fluids, get plenty of rest, and stop watching Marcus Welby."

* * *

The doctor told this guy to stop playing golf. "The way you look, you shouldn't take a chance getting so close to that hole in the ground."

PROFOUND

*Think of how smart we all would be,
if we retained as much of what we read
as of what we eat!*

* * *

If you don't think there is strength in numbers,
consider the fragile snowflake. If enough of them
stick together, they can paralyze the whole city.

* * *

Luck is the idol of the idle.

* * *

One measure of intelligence is the length of time it
takes you to get to your wit's end.

* * *

You can get something for nothing — like about
10 years if you don't pay your income tax.

Knowledge is knowing the fact that fire will burn.
Wisdom is remembering the blister.

* * *

Anybody who keeps a chip on his shoulder isn't
chopping much wood.

* * *

Some people are like wheelbarrows, trailers and
canoes. They need to be pushed, pulled or paddled.

* * *

This is a lollipop world. Everybody's trying
to get their licks in.

* * *

If the going is getting easier, you are not climbing.

* * *

Some men remind one of blisters. They don't
show up until the work is done.

* * *

If you can tell the difference between good advice
and bad advice — you don't need advice.

* * *

Life has a way of balancing things. We are down-
hearted because we don't get everything we want,
and happy because we don't get what we deserve.

* * *

"If work is a virtue, some people are living in sin."

Religion

The Lord loveth a cheerful giver!
He also accepteth from a grouch.

* * *

New religion for those who have really had it . . .
It'll be called: "THE FIRST CHURCH OF THE
LAST STRAW."

* * *

SELF IMAGE

When the Lord gave out looks, I thought He said
    books. I didn't want any.
When He gave out ears, I thought He said beers.
    I ordered two large ones.
When He gave out noses, I thought He said roses.
    I ordered a big red one.
Lord, I'm a mess!

67

Two old maid sisters were living together. One night one of them said in her prayers:

"Dear Lord, I ask nothing for myself; but please send my sister a brother-in-law."

* * *

Minister dickering with dealer for a new car. They had gotten fairly close together, but were still several dollars apart.

"Come on now, you can do better than that. I'm just a POOR Baptist preacher."

"I know, I've heard you preach."

* * *

"Adultry is as bad as murder! Isn't it Mrs. Smith?" cried the evangelist.

"I don't know," she replied, "I've never killed anybody."

* * *

The priest was trying to get Kelly, the old drunk to reform, but was having no luck. One day Kelly said: "Tell me, Father. What is sciatica?"

The priest seized the opportunity to throw a scare into Kelly. "Sciatica is a very painful affliction usually caused by too much to drink and a self-indulgent life."

"Is that so?" Kelly responded.

"Why do you ask?" said Father.

"I just read in the papers that the Bishop is going back into the hospital. It seems he suffers from chronic sciatica."

The world is so full of problems that, if Moses came down from Mount Sinai today, two of the tablets he would be carrying would be aspirin.

* * *

Sunday School teacher: "Why do you love God?"
Little child: "I don't know, but I guess maybe it just runs in our family."

* * *

In Sunday school, Jennifer, a seven year old girl, was telling her classmates the wonderful Bible story of David and Goliath. After Jennifer had finished the story, the teacher asked the class what the story had taught them — and one little girl answered, "Duck!"

* * *

Mean man makes obscene phone calls: He calls up Christian Scientists and says, "Penicillin, bufferin, cortisone, aspirin . . . !"

* * *

Between the Ecumenical Movement and Women's Lib, someday we'll be going into a Catholic Church and saying, "Good morning, Father Zelda."

* * *

Adam and Eve had their marital problems just like any other couple. One day Adam really got angry. "Dammit!" he yelled at Eve, "You've put my shorts in the salad again!"

Two ministers of different faiths were good friends but disagreed on religious issues. After a heated discussion, one said to the other: "That's all right. We'll just agree to disagree. The thing that counts is that we're both doing the Lord's work — you in your way and I in His."

* * *

Sunday school teacher testing her pupils knowledge of proverbs: "Cleanliness is next to what?" she asked a little boy. "Impossible."

* * *

Sunday school teacher: "Lot was warned to take his wife and flee out of the city but his wife looked back and was turned to salt." A little girl raised her hand and asked, "I was wondering what happened to his flea?"

* * *

As the minister began his Sunday sermon, there was a loud clap of thunder signaling the start of a downpour. "Isn't that just like the Lord?" he said. "Here we are sitting and relaxing and He's out there washing our cars."

* * *

Rabbi defending cause to his Christian friend: "Your entire religion is based on ours. You even took the Ten Commandments from us."

"True," said the Christian, "but you sure can't say we kept them."

SALES

LET'S PUT THE "SALES" BACK IN SALESMAN

SHARES—*Ideas, experiences, know-how , prospects*
ADAPTS—*Circumstances, interruptions, moods*
LABORS—*Discipline, detail, follow-thru*
EMPATHIZES—*Wants and needs, problems*
SENSES—*Pride, integrity*
MANAGER—*Attitudes, decisions, territory, time*
ASKS—*Info, involvement, dialogue, help, initiative*
NEWS—*Benefits, markets, components, savings, uses*

* * *

A lady walked into an appliance store and asked to see some toasters. A high pressure salesman decided that instead of a toaster, he would sell her an expensive freezer.

"Madam, believe me, when I tell you this freezer will pay for itself in no time . . ."

"Fine, as soon as it does, send it over."

Salesman snowed in by blizzard, wired the home office: "I can't get out of my hotel room in this small town for two weeks. —Stop — I cannot sell anything. — Stop — What shall I do? — Stop —

Home office replied: "Start your vacation immediately!"

* * *

"Don't bother to open your case," the purchasing agent said to the salesman.

"Please, let me, I haven't seen what's in it for two weeks myself."

* * *

An insurance agent said to a new client, "I want to sell this policy, but I'm not like 'other' insurance agents. I'm 'not' going to frighten or scare you into buying it. So take the policy home and sleep on it tonight and IF you wake up in the morning, give me a call."

* * *

The new traveling salesman was chatting with an oldtimer on the road, who asked him how he was doing.

"Not so good," said the new man. "Everyplace I go, I get insulted."

"That's funny," said the oldtimer. "I've been traveling for more than forty years and I've had my samples pitched out the door, been thrown out myself, kicked down stairs, and was even punched in the nose once — but, I was never insulted.

72

Salesmen who frequent restaurants that feature topless waitresses are called "chestnuts"!

* * *

The lady went into the shoe store to buy a pair of loafers. The manager said to her, "Yes, we have quite a selection of loafers. I'll see if I can get one to wait on you."

* * *

Enterprising salesman with new and undisguised sales weapon: The salesman had a homing pigeon delivered by Western Union messenger. Tied to the pigeon's leg was a tag which stated: "If you want to know more about our product, throw our representative out the window."

* * *

The president of a dog food company called a meeting of all his salesmen and at the start of the meeting asked: "Who has the best dog food?"

He pointed at one of his employees and the man said emphatically: "We have!"

He pointed at another and the answer was the same.

After getting a convincing "ours" from several of the men, he asked: "Well, if ours is the best, why is it not selling?"

All was quiet for a long time. Then finally, a little fellow in the back row held up his hand: "I can tell you why it isn't selling . . the dogs won't eat it."

Manager said to a fired salesman: "In a way, though, I'll be sorry to lose you. You've been like a son to me — insolent, surly, and unappreciative!"

* * *

The boss who was heckled by his slightly loaded salesman: "Tomorrow when you go out, I hope you fill your order book before you lose it!"

* * *

A salesman was explaining to a friend the reason for his sudden prosperity.

"I sell ladies hosiery," he said, "Sometimes, if the woman of the house wants me to, I put them on for her."

"You sure must sell a lot of hose that way," said his friend.

"No," the salesman said, "my legs look lousy in women's hose."

* * *

A new salesman in the Northwest had snow tires put on the company car at the first sign of winter. These tires proved inadequate in an ice storm. He stopped at the first garage to buy chains. The manager noticed the tires were designed to hold studs and suggested they would be better than chains. So, he had the studs installed.

There was a considerable reaction from the company bookkeeper over the entry on his expense account under "miscellaneous expenses" upon his return. It read: "Stud Service for company car."

SIGNS OF THE TIMES

Donut Shop for Sale — Owner in the Hole!

* * *

Supermarket sign stated: "Wanted — clerk to work 8 hours a day to replace one who didn't."

* * *

Train takes 14 seconds to go thru this crossing whether your car is on the tracks or not.

* * *

Courthouse clerk put this sign over the marriage license window at lunch time: "Be back at 1:00 o'clock — think it over!"

* * *

Sign above door of a small drive in market: "This place is guarded by shotgun three nights a week — you guess which nights."

A maternity shop had this sign in the front window: "Hatching Frocks"

* * *

Out to Lunch!
If Not Back By 5
Out to Dinner, Also

* * *

Seen on a laundry truck: "We don't mangle your clothes by machinery. We do it by hand."

* * *

Sign on a service station/restaurant:
"EAT HERE and GET GAS."

* * *

A truck from a nursery with a sign on the back reading: "A lawn without a tree, ain't fit for a dog."

* * *

"Going Out Of Business!
WE UNDERSOLD EVERYONE!!"

* * *

From a fortune cookie in a Chinese restaurant:
"Disregard previous cookie."

* * *

A night club proprietor crowded the joint by advertising: "Thirteen beautiful girls — twelve beautiful costumes."

Speaking

"Mr. Chairman, I truly admire your introduction and your wonderful way with words. I especially admire the way you do not let the facts interfere with what you have to say."

* * *

At a political convention, a sign had been erected near the speaker's platform for the benefit of the press photographers. It read: "Do not photograph the speakers while they are addressing the audience. Shoot them as they approach platform."

* * *

Lecturer: "Who was braver than Lancelot, wiser than Socrates, more truthful than George Washington, more honorable than Lincoln, wittier than Mark Twain and more handsome than Apollo?" From the rear of the audience came: "My wife's first husband."

"You know, at my last performance, I had the audience glued to their seats," boasted an actor whose talent was far exceeded by his conceit.

"Really?" replied the co-star. "How very clever of you to think of it."

* * *

A woman, who traveled around the country lecturing on safety, always practiced what she preached. She once arrived at a strange hotel and thought she had better check the location of the fire escape. She started looking for it. She came to an unmarked door and opened it, only to find that it was a bathroom. The tub was occupied by a rather heavy-set old fellow.

"Oh, excuse me," she said, "I was just looking for the fire escape."

As she turned and walked down the hall, she heard the patter of bare feet. She turned around to see the refugee from the bathroom, draped in a towel and running after her and shouting, "Wait for me. Wait for me. Where's the fire?"

* * *

The executive was so nervous and worried about the speech he had to make, that he had butterflies in his stomach. Turning to the chairman, he told him of his nervousness. The chairman advised, "Here, take this aspirin and the butterflies will go away." The executive moaned in reply. "I already took an aspirin and the butterflies are playing ping-pong with it!"

SPORTS

A young wife was telling a friend about the fight she had with her husband. " . . . and then he picked up and left home," she wailed.

"Oh, don't let that bother you, he's done that before."

"Yes, but this time he took his golf clubs."

* * *

Notorious horse player looked like he had just lost his best friend. "Hey, Jackie, what's wrong?" "I had $500 stashed away to bet on the ponies today and would you believe . . . my wife found it and blew it all on rent and groceries."

* * *

"A fellow complained that he went to Wrigley Field Stadium on Bat Day and got a bat; went on Cap Day and got a cap; went on Ladies Day and was disappointed.

"One GOOD reason why I don't play golf is because I have enough crises in my life without volunteering for 18 of them on my day off."

* * *

Owner of a race horse asked a jockey why he didn't ride his mount thru a hole when it opened in the final turn. "Sir, did you ever try to go thru a hole that was going faster than your horse?"

* * *

Promising high school basketball player was asked: "Are you in the top half of your class?" "No, sir," he replied, "I'm one of those who make the top half POSSIBLE."

* * *

The basketball star was in danger of flunking out of school. A special test was given orally by the dean as a last attempt to pass him. His coach accompanied the star to the test to give encouragement. The dean asked: "How much is eight times seven?"

"Fifty," replied the star.

"Wrong," said the dean, "I'm sorry, but I can't pass you."

"Aw, dean," said the coach, "Come on. He only missed by two."

* * *

Fish may be dumb, but no one has ever seen one buy five hundred dollars worth of equipment to hook a man.

80

Transportation

The jet age can be defined as —
breakfast in London, lunch in New York,
dinner in San Francisco,
and baggage in Buenos Aires.

* * *

I never have any luck when I travel by air. One flight I took was so rough, everybody on the plane was sick, including Paul Newman . . . and he was in the movie.

* * *

A man was complaining that he just bought a prefab house and it cost him $50,000.

"Isn't that an awful lot to pay for a prefab house?"

"Yes, it wasn't that much to begin with . . . but I told the factory I wanted it right away and they sent it to me airmail!"

That airline I just came in on is so small, they dusted the crops on the way.

* * *

If you think the skies are friendly, you should see what's going on in the terminals.

* * *

There's still a bit of risk in aviation. The taxi ride from the city to the airport.

* * *

I don't fly on account of my religion . . . . I'm a devout coward.

* * *

"Look, the people way down there look like ants."
"They are ants. Our plane is still on the runway!"

* * *

United stewie reports that she is looking for two things in a prospective husband . . . rich parents!

* * *

A couple of college girls were talking about their future plans. One said she planned to get a job as an airline hostess.

"That way," she said, "I'll meet lots of men."

"That might be a good idea," agreed her friend, "but wouldn't you meet just as many men working at some other job?"

"Maybe," she said, "but not strapped down."

TV is an appliance
which changes children from
irresistible forces to immovable objects.

* * *

Children who watch TV every night will go down
in history . . . not to mention arithmetic, science
spelling . . .

* * *

A man who watches football on television
every Sunday said, "I've seen a lot of instant replays
but it hasn't bothered me, hasn't bothered me, hasn't
bothered me . . ."

* * *

Television rating outfit phoned a thousand men to
ask: "What are you listening to right now?" 83%
replied: "My wife."

When you see Mr. Whipple get excited over squeezing the Charmin, it makes you wonder what Mrs. Whipple looks like!

* * *

TV weather forecasting is becoming more accurate. But it's still several hours behind arthritis.

* * *

Why is it that scientists can make adjustments on a space vehicle winging thousands of miles out in space, but the TV repairman has to take MY set to the shop?

* * *

The new bride is very upset with television. She says: "The trouble with TV is, it's either sex or violence."

I said: "What do you mean sex or violence?"

She said: "If you turn it on, it's violence. If you turn it off, it's sex."

* * *

Soap operas are marvelous! One show is about an alcoholic, a murderer, a two-timing husband, an embezzler, a teenager on drugs, an unfaithful wife, a child molester, and an unmarried mother. Know what it is called? "Just Plain Folks."

* * *

Some people dislike TV so much that they sit up all night staring at it.

84

TRUE FAVORITES

Laugh, and the world laughs with you;
Weep, and you weep alone.
For the sad old earth must borrow its mirth,
But has trouble enough of its own.
Sing, and hills will answer;
Sigh, and its lost on the air.
The echoes bound to a joyful sound,
But shrink from voicing care.

* * *

Laughter is a silver shield
   To put on every day
It releases many tensions;
   Heartaches fly away.

* * *

Nothing is easier than fault-finding: no talent, no
self-denial, no brains, no character are required to
set up in the grumbling business.

A MONKEY'S VIEWPOINT

Three monkeys dining in a cocoanut tree
Were discussing something they thought shouldn't
   be,
Said one to the others, "Now listen, you two —
Here monkeys, is something that cannot be true:
"That humans descend from our noble race.
Why, it's shocking — a terrible disgrace.
Whoever heard of a monkey deserting his wife;
Leaving a baby to starve; maybe ruin its life?

"And have you ever known of a mother monk
To leave her darling with strangers to bunk?
Human babies are handed from one to another
And some scarcely know the love of a mother.
"I've never known a monkey so selfish to be
As to build a fence 'round a cocoanut tree
So other monkeys couldn't get a wee taste
While bushels of cocoanuts were going to waste.

"Why, if I'd put a fence 'round this cocoanut tree,
Starvation would force you to steal food from me.
And here is another thing a monkey won't do:
Seek a cocktail parlor and get on a stew;

"Carouse, or whoopee, disgracing his life,
Then reel madly home and beat up his wife.
Some humans think it fun — they fuss and
      they cuss —
They've descended from something, but it can't
      be from us."

86

PRAYER

I know not by what methods rare,
But this I know — God answers prayer.
I know not when He sends the word.
that tells us fervent prayer is heard
I know it cometh — soon or late;
Therefore we need to pray and wait
I know not if the blessings sought
Will come in just the way I thought
I leave my prayers with Him alone,
Whose Will is wiser than my own!

* * *

We have tried to bring peace in our world. We have tried with guns, ships, planes and rockets. We have tried with food, farm machinery, medicine, and clothes. But we have failed. There are two ways to secure a lasting peace. One is to destroy it completely so there would not any longer be a world. The other way to bring peace to our world is for you and me and everyone else to be filled with the mind and spirit and character of the Galilean Carpenter. That seems childish to a good many. It is too simple for some and too complicated for others. Sherman was right. War is Hell. But the Carpenter was also right, "Peace I leave with you, my peace I give to you." We have tried every way to find peace except THE way. Maybe one day before we blow ourselves to pieces we will try HIS way. We will never know peace in the world till He who made it rules it, and us, not thru force but by love.

HOW TO MEASURE THE WORTH OF A MAN OR A WOMAN!

Not 'how did he die?' but 'how did he live?'
Not what did he gain . . what did he give . . .
Not what was his station. Had he a heart.
How did he play his God-fearing part.
Was he ever ready with words of cheer . . .
to bring back a smile . . . to banish a tear.
Not what was his church nor what was his creed
but had he befriended those really in need.
Not what did the sketch in the newspaper say
but how many were sorry when he passed away.

* * *

No one really escapes criticism, and the more eminent one is the more criticism may be expected. It is, as Addison said in his essay on Censure, folly to think of escaping it and weakness to be affected by it.

* * *

PROCRASTINATION
Procrastination is my sin.
It brings me naught but sorrow.
I know that I should stop it.
In fact, I will . . . tomorrow!

* * *

The man who wants to lead the orchestra must turn his back upon the crowd.

HUMOR

Give me a sense of humor
Give me the grace to see a joke
To get some happiness from life
And pass it on to other folk.

* * *

Failure should be our teacher, not our undertaker. It should challenge us to new heights of accomplishment, not pull us to new depths of despair. Failure is delay, but not defeat. It is a temporary detour, not a dead-end street.

* * *

Albert Einstein said: *"Strange is our situation here upon earth. Each of us comes for a short visit, not knowing why yet sometimes seeming to divine a purpose. From the standpoint of daily life, there is one thing we do know; that man is here for the sake of other men — above all for those upon whose smiles and well-being our own happiness depends, and also for the countless unknown souls with whose fate we are connected by a bond of sympathy: Many times a day I realize how much my own outer and inner life is built upon the labor of my fellow men, both living and dead, and how earnestly I must exert myself in order to give in return as much as I have received. My peace of mind is often troubled by the depressing sense that I have borrowed too heavily from the work of other men."*

89

GET A TRANSFER

If you are on the gloomy line
Get a transfer
Don't travel where they fret and whine
Get a transfer
Get off the track of doubt and gloom
Get on the sunshine track, there's room
Get a transfer
If you're on the worry train
Get a transfer
You must not stay there and complain
Get a transfer
The cheerful cars are passing thru
And there is lots of room for you
Get a transfer
If you're on the grouchy track
Get a transfer
Just take a happy special back
Get a transfer
Jump on the train and pull the rope
That lands you at the station Hope
Get a transfer.

* * *

CRITICISM

Don't fear criticism — Galleries are full of critics.
They play no ball, fight no fights. Make no mistakes
because they attempt nothing. Down in the arena
are doers. They make mistakes because they attempt things.

90

LOVE FOR A VERY SPECIAL CHILD

A meeting was held quite far from earth
"It's time again for another birth."
said the angels to the Lord above,
"This special child will need much love.
His progress may seem very slow,
Accomplishments he may not show,
and he'll require extra care from the folks
he meets way down there.

"He may not run or laugh or play,
His thoughts may seem quite far away
In many ways he won't adapt,
And he'll be known as handicapped.

"So let's be careful where he's sent,
We want his life to be content.
Please, Lord, find the parents who
Will do a special job for You.

"They will not realize right away,
The leading role they're asked to play,
But with this child sent from above
Comes stronger faith and richer love.

"And soon they'll know the privilege given
In caring for this human gift from Heaven
This precious charge, so meek and mild
Is God's uniquely special child!"

* * *

Lord, I ain't what I ought to be,
I ain't what I want to be,
I ain't what I'm going to be,
But, thank the Lord,
I ain't what I used to be.

* * *

CRITICIZE

Man is the only creature capable of finding fault and then doing something about it. Man is the only creature endowed with talent for constructive criticism. Instead of creating all things in a finished state and making man complete in all knowledge and skills, the Creator gave humanity the desire and the ability to: (1) Improve, discover and then invent, (2) To envision better things, (3) To achieve them.

That is the foundation of criticism, which is the builder of civilization. It was constructive criticism- intelligent faultfinding which brought man out of caves and jungles of primitive times into the present state of a civilized society.

It was the desire for something better that improved shelter, food, clothing, transportation, communication, lighting, in short, the comforts of life.

Criticism laid the groundwork for democracy and criticism makes it possible for democracy to survive.

THE ANONYMOUS GREAT

Only in headline situations is the spotlight turned on the inner qualities that add up to greatness. More often such qualities go unrecognized and this is tremendously encouraging. It means that ordinary people living inconspicuous lives, can qualify for greatness, too.

Persons who are bearing burdens uncomplainingly, the courageous ill and handicapped . . . and those who do the distasteful jobs of caring for them . . . cheerfully . . . these are great after their fashion. As are people who have ample cause for bitterness, yet are not bitter. And others to whom disappointment and heartbreak have come repeatedly, but who refuse to let their faith be shattered. And those faced with terrifying situations, with spirit-shaking fears, yet who somehow manage to keep their flags flying. These . . . and others like them . . . are the anonymous great among us.

* * *

Man's greatest search is to search for freedom. Freedom from his own selfish, animal, egotistical, conniving, inquisitive, passionate nature — he is free from this; and his greatest thing to avoid is loneliness. Not being alone, but loneliness. The feeling that nobody really cares whether he gets up in the morning or not are tied in with love. Man wants to love something and wants something to love him.

GREATNESS

Greatness! Everyone, in his own way seeks it. Few find it. Those that do, hardly ever recognize it. We all want to be great. The mistake comes in the manner in which we seek it. We get it mixed with fame and fortune and power. We have a lingering thought in the back of our mind, that unless we achieve the fame, fortune and power, we haven't made it. We aren't great. We are just a nobody. That is where the Nazarene comes in. One of the basic things that Galilean does for those whose lives He changes is to put greatness within their reach.

Real greatness doesn't lie in those things we have always thought it does. Money, fame, and power cannot make us great. Those who rank on the horizon of history as great men, for the most part, lacked those things. Lincoln was a great man. What made Lincoln great was his service. The Carpenter put it: "The greatest among you shall be your servant." This might help some of us, if all our elected officials could catch a glimpse of the wisdom of that statement. What a nation we'd have. Some of the greatest people that ever lived never made the headlines, held office, or owned an acre of land. They were just plain, common, ordinary people whose lives came under the influence of the Fisher of Men. He got His hold on them and He made them great. They became servants . . . great servants. That Galilean was a great man. Great enough to bow low and wash the feet of His fellow men. You know, I guess, we grow tall by bending low.

LOVE BEATITUDES FOR THE
FRIENDS OF THE HANDICAPPED

BLESSED ARE YOU:

Who take time to listen to difficult speech, for you help us to know that if we persevere we can be understood.

Who walk with us in public . . . and ignore stares of strangers for in your companionship we find havens of relaxation.

Who never bid us to "hurry up" and more blessed are you who do not snatch our tasks from our hands to do them for us, for often we need time rather than help.

Who stand beside us as we enter new and untried ventures, for our failure will be outweighed by the times we surprise ourselves and you,

Who ask for our help, for our greatest need is to be needed.

* * *

YOUR MOST PRECIOUS BEQUEST

Overheard two businessmen commiserating with each other about the painful bite taxes are taking out of their incomes. "In my racket," said one, "you make a lot of money but what good does it do you? It takes every dollar I make to run my house and pay my taxes. I'll never be able to leave anything to my children." It was rather obvious that if either of them did leave their children anything it would be ONLY money.

One cannot read a biography without being impressed by the hard fact that many promising young people have never amounted to much. Chiefly because their parents saw to it that they didn't HAVE to.

The most precious thing you can leave YOUR children is not likely to be mentioned in your WILL.

* * *

My hands were busy thru the day . . .
I didn't have much time to play
the little games you asked me to . . .
I didn't have much time for you.

I'd wash your clothes,
I'd sew and cook, but when you'd bring
your picture book and ask me to share your fun —
I'd say "A little later son."

But life is short, and years rush past
and little boys grow up fast —
no longer is he at your side
his precious secrets to confide.

The picture books are put away
there aren't any games left to play —
no good night kiss, no prayers to hear —
that all belongs to yesteryear.

My hands once busy now lie still
the days are long and hard to fill
Gee I wish I might go back and do . . .
the little things you asked me to.

The reason the weaker sex is the stronger sex —
is because of the weakness of the stronger sex
for the weaker sex.

* * *

"Always been a woman telling me when to be home," a man complained to his psychiatrist.

"First it was my mother, then my wife, now the baby sitter."

* * *

My wife has finally solved the riddle as to why God created man and then woman. She says, "He did it that way because He didn't want any advice while creating man."

* * *

"The only woman who wishes she were a year older is the one who is expecting a baby."

I never realized how gullible women were until I saw this sign in a beauty parlor: SHAMPOO $5. REAL POO $10.

* * *

Women need never expect to be mens' equals until they sport a large bald spot on top of their heads and still think they are handsome.

* * *

Churchill was asked, "What do you say to the prediction that in the year 2000, women will be ruling the world?" Answer: "They still will, eh?"

* * *

Husband: "Stupid, just plain stupid, the way women spend money. I never saw such silly spending."

"Okay," said wife, "maybe so, but one thing you never saw. You never saw a woman buy a bottle of hair restorer from a 'baldheaded' barber."

* * *

Why women are called the opposite sex. If a man thinks he's fooling one of them, he soon finds that the facts are just the opposite.

* * *

A woman tourist posed for a picture in front of some fallen pillars in Greece. "Don't get the car in the picture," she warned, "or my husband will think I ran into the place!"

"Charles," demanded his wife, "do you think I'm going to wear this old muskrat coat all my life?"

"Why not, dear?" he replied, "The muskrats do."

* * *

Hurricanes are like tornadoes, except they have bigger eyes, longer lashes, broader bases and are more devastating. That's why they are given girl's names.

* * *

Martha was complaining to her husband.

"Look at the old clothes I wear, you cheapskate. Why, if anyone came to visit us, they would think I was your cook."

"Not if they stayed for dinner," was her husband's terse reply.

* * *

My wife is sneaky. She figured out a way to get me to take out the garbage every day. She puts it in my golf bag!

* * *

The office Don Juan lost no time in trying to impress the new secretary, a young and pretty girl. He told her about his feats on the college football team, the dance floor, during the war, and every other line of activity he could think of. After a wearisome recital of his achievements, the girl gave him a wide-eyed smile, asking, "Have you ever had a group photograph taken of yourself?"

Women are like an abstract painting. A man will never get to like it if he tries to understand it.

* * *

"Your typing is really improving, Miss Jones. Only three mistakes." "Now," he snarled, "type the second word."

* * *

Her clothes are like barbed wire. They protect the property without obstructing the view.

* * *

My wife has always been a firm believer in re-cycling, only she calls it by a different name — garage sales.

* * *

Hear about the woman who was sent to the hospital with a bad case of exhaustion. She overworked her-self trying to use every labor saving gadget in her kitchen!

* * *

I marvel at how my wife can thread a needle! I grit my teeth when she tries to put the car into the garage.

* * *

The football widow's husband wouldn't leave the TV set to look at her until she got a nightgown made of Astroturf.

Two times when men are baffled by women: Before and after marriage.

* * *

Mother at front door ready to go to church, her arms full of coats and hats for three little ones. Husband: "Okay, let's get going." She handed him the coats and hats. "All right, this time you put the kids coats and hats on them and I'll go out and honk the horn."

* * *

Young lady to her friend: "The man I marry must shine in company, be musical, tell jokes, sing, dance and stay home nights."

Friend: "You don't want a husband. You want a television set."

* * *

If a man thinks for a moment that he can understand women, he has it timed about right.

* * *

Husband to loquacious wife: "You are just like a broken old umbrella you just can't shut up."

Wife: "How right you are. I am like an old umbrella. A bunch of ribs, covered with rags and tied to an old stick."

* * *

Some girls, like golf balls, get a lot of distance out of their dimples.

Heard a woman ask a cop who stopped her for going thru a red light: "If you give me a ticket, will it count against me when I apply for a driver's license?"

* * *

"My wife has a very bad memory."
"Forgets everything?"
"No, she remembers everything!"

* * *

Pregnant women miss little attentions from their husbands. One woman turns on the tea kettle just to hear it whistle.

* * *

On a crowded street, a motorist stopped suddenly for a red light and his rear bumper was bashed by the car behind. The driver got out, looked over the damage, glared at the woman driving the other auto, returned to his car and roared off.

At the next light, the same thing happened. Finally, after the third bump, the woman got out of her car and came over, holding out her driver's license and other credentials.

"Look, madam," said the victim helplessly, "never mind that stuff. All I want from you is a five minute start."

* * *

"Yes, men may be more intelligent than women. But you never see a woman marrying a dumb man because of his shape."

102

No matter what excellent imitations science produces, they can never take the place of the real thing. Few men pay any attention to bathing suits on store window dummies.

* * *

He was a bit shy, and after she had thrown her arms around him and kissed him for bringing her a bouquet of roses, he arose and started to leave.

"I'm sorry I offended you," she said.

"Oh, I'm not offended," he replied. "I'm going for more roses."

* * *

Man, finding himself suddenly and unexpectedly at the Pearly Gates: "Good Heavens, how did I get here?"

Saint Peter said: "Don't you remember your wife saying — Be an angel and let me drive?"

* * *

An innocent looking old lady cashed a check at the super market and thanked the cashier. "I just don't know what I'd do without you people now that the bank has stopped cashing my checks."

* * *

What my wife knows about cars can be put in a thimble. One day she came to me and said, "I want you to look at the car. I washed the windows, I emptied the ash tray, I swept the carpet, and I dusted the cushions and STILL it won't start."

A cruel wife told her husband: "You sure made a prize fool of yourself tonight. It's a good thing that people didn't realize you were sober."

* * *

"Sammy, I want to ask you a question."
"Anything, darling."
"Tell me. If you had never met me would you have loved me just the same?"

* * *

A group of skydivers leap from their plane yelling "Geronimo!" — except for the Women's Libber who yelled, "Pocahontas!"

* * *

One night Dad got into a swinging match with the milkman. A third man was caught up in the fight and a three way slugfest ensued. Police arrived and the trio was taken to jail and booked. Dad was given an added demerit for carrying a gun without a license. He liked to carry a pistol altho he never used it.

The three were not released until morning, and the first thing Dad did was call mother.
"Where have you been?"
"In jail."
"What for?"
"Disturbing the peace, destroying property, resisting arrest and carrying a gun without a license."
"Oh, thank God! I thought you were with another woman."

YOUNG ADULT

Twenty years ago we were told
we weren't as smart as our parents.
Today we're not as smart as our kids.
Where did we go wrong?

* * *

Two college boys were walking down the street. "You know, man," said one, "I'm really worried."

"What's the problem?" his friend inquired.

"Well, last night I was talking to my parents, and I'm beginning to see my old man's point of view."

* * *

Little girl showing some friends thru her home: "This is my room, this is my brother's room, and this is," opening the bathroom door and pointing to the scale "where my mother measures her feet."

Girl Friend: "My dad is an engineer. He takes things apart to see why they don't go."

Boy Friend: "So what?"

Girl Friend: "So, you'd better go."

* * *

"Does anyone know what a cannibal is?" asked the teacher. No response. "John, do you know what a cannibal is?" "No, ma'am." "Well," said the teacher, "If you were to eat your mother and father, what would you be?" "An orphan, ma'am," was John's irrefutable reply.

* * *

A schoolteacher was teaching the second grade. "What's the opposite of misery?" she asked a little girl.

"Joy," the girl said quickly.

"That's right," the teacher said. "Now, what's the opposite of sorrow?" she asked another little girl.

"Happiness," she said.

"Right," the teacher said. "Now what's the opposite of woe?" she asked a little boy.

"Giddyap!" he said.

* * *

Young people haven't really changed much from when we were young. They still grow up, go to school, get a job, get married and have children. The difference is they don't necessarily do it in that order.

There is one thing about children. They never go around showing pictures of their grandparents.

* * *

"Do you mind if I take the car tonight?" a father asked his son. "I'm taking your mother to the movies and I want to impress her."

* * *

At the movies one youngster turned to the other and said, "I must be growing up. The love scenes don't make me sick anymore."

* * *

Mother: "You don't have to be afraid of going to the hospital to have your tonsils out."
Little Boy: "I'm not afraid, but I'm not gonna let 'em palm a baby off on me like they did you. I want a beagle pup."

* * *

The young son watched his father finish a big dinner and then loosen his belt. "Look, mommy," he exclaimed. "Dad's just moved his decimal point over 2 places."

* * *

Small boy lowered his head at dinner table one night and told his parents there was to be a small PTA meeting the next day. "Well, if it is just a small one do you think we ought to go?" "I'm afraid so, it is just you, me and the principal."

Hear about the kid who put on a clean pair of sox every day and by the end of the week he couldn't get his shoes on?

* * *

A friend complained that he can't communicate with his son. "How can you have a man to man talk with someone who is wearing an earring?"

* * *

Young boy admiring Dobermans at Dog Show. A message came over the loud speaker. "Will John Kershaw, age 7, please report to the Secretary's tent." With a look of disgust, the boy turned to the exhibitor and said, "Damn it, I must have got lost again." — and disappeared into the crowd.

* * *

Teacher to first grader: "Have you ever had measles or chicken pox?"
"No, but I've had Rice Krispies."

* * *

Conversation overheard involving 2 five year olds:
She: "Let's play pregnant."
He: "Okay, how do you play pregnant?"
She: "It's easy. We both go in the bathroom. You shave and I throwup."

* * *

"Dad, I'm 16 now, so please treat me like an adult."
"Okay, here's the phone bill."

108

One mother giving her son a lecture about his use of four-letter words. "But mom, Norman Mailer uses words like that all the time."

"Well, if that's where you're getting it, I don't want you to play with him anymore."

* * *

A husband to his wife as he gazed at a picture of himself with their college student son.

"Wouldn't it look more natural if he had his hand in my pocket?"

* * *

A note left by a 10 year old and found by his mother when she returned from shopping. "I am having a very bad headache and stomachache. I have taken two aspirins and a glass of milk and gone out to play football."

* * *

"What's the best way to teach a girl to swim?" asked Bud.

"That requires technique," answered Bob. "First you put your left arm around her waist. Then you gently take her left hand and . . ."

"She's my sister," said Bud.

"Oh! Then just push her off the dock."

* * *

One of the neighbor kids offered to rake up the leaves for $2 an hour — or $4, if he had to listen to how hard we had it as a boy.

A six year old was looking at the pictures of his parents wedding. His father described the ceremony and tried to explain the meaning of the wedding. Suddenly the light dawned!

"Oh, is that when you got mother to come to work for us?"

* * *

Kindergarten teacher asked new arrival what his father's name was. "Daddy." "No, I mean his first name. What does your mother call him?" "She doesn't call him anything, she likes him."

* * *

A small boy in a department store was standing near the escalator watching the moving handrail.

"Something wrong?" asked a saleslady.

"Nope! Just waiting for my chewing gum to come back."

* * *

He's got a clean mind — ain't never been used.

* * *

"Teacher," said little Bertie, "I can't do this problem because I ain't got no pencils."

"Now, Bertie," she said, "It's a pencil. 'We don't have any pencils.' 'They don't have any pencils.' Do you understand?"

"No," admitted Bertie. "What happened to all them pencils."

A small boy on the verge of being spanked asked mother if she was spanked by her mother when she was a little girl. Receiving an affirmative answer, he asked, "And did grandmother's grandmother spank her, too?" Another nod. "Gee, isn't it about time we stopped this chain of brutality?"

* * *

Overheard one boy ask another: "What's the meaning of spunk?"
"That's after your Dad spanks you. — You're spunk."

* * *

Teenager to father hidden behind newspaper: "I know you're listening. Your knuckles are white."

* * *

If It's "LAUGHTER" Your After

DO: . . .

read through these humor items again. Underline or mark those that appeal to you and then go back through the book frequently to reread your selected items. By so doing, you'll discover these items become planted in your sub-concious and later emerge at very opportune moments as impressive off-hand ad-libs.

Take advantage of the many obvious sources of additional humor idea material. Your local library and book stores have numerous volumes devoted to humor, laughter, wit and comedy. To help you in this regard I have listed some suggestions for timely, weekly material available now.

Start your own humor collection of situations in which people have used humor as a tactical weapon. All too often such material is simply dumped into a drawer or box, but if your intentions are serious, you'll need some kind of organization. Start now to record your Sense of Humor concepts and items on 3 x 5 cards, and then file them under key subject areas or categories that interest you specifically. Before long you'll begin to realize that this categorizing is a very personal thing and almost every item you decide to save can be put in a variety of areas. Consequently, cross-referencing is very helpful and this can easily be accomplished by using No-Carbon-Required (NCR) duplicate copy paper available from most printers and can be cut to 3 x 5 size. Copying machines can also serve this purpose. Most material will benefit from your tightening and condensing efforts, however, when you record material for your files be sure the essentials of time, place, and characterization are included in order to set the scene properly. Keep in mind that effective punch lines are usually a culmination of a precisely worded, carefully created continuity, and it's these specific lines that set up the punch lines. If this foundation is missing, your punch lines will fall as flat as the roof of a house whose bricks are improperly laid.

Your personal Sense of Humor treasury benefits you greatly because as you read, clip and categorize, you draw information into yourself and begin to acquire the essence of a Sense of Humor. You'll be exposing yourself to imaginative situations and to the ideas and attitudes of people whose use of their Sense of Humor will inspire you. You'll gain a real appreciation of story structure, flow and continuity. You won't have to hunt for point-making examples; your sub-conscious will volunteer them because through file-building you've imbedded them there. Some ideas you'll borrow, and, many will be suggested by your own humorous encounters, but all your efforts will contribute to that seemingly spontaneous ad-lib and your file will prove to be a priceless investment. It's often said that a person with an operating Sense of Humor is a person who has a trained memory, and hopes other people haven't.

After assembling your categorized cards, the creation of a chunk or vignette is achieved by lifting choice items from your file, spreading them on a large table, changing

114

their sequence pattern until you strike the most comfortable continuity. Draw upon your imagination and creativity for filling in the gaps, smoothly tying your stories together.

In trying to anticipate your need for beginning material, I have provided many items classed as one-liners. A one-liner is usually any humor situation which uses as few words as possible and ends with a unique twist, phrase, or punchline. These capitalize on the fact that many people have difficulty maintaining interest in anything that fails to be short, snappy, and loaded with excitement. It's hoped that from these you'll gain a better idea of what's involved in producing the kind of instant ad-lib or vignette or chunk that has become so popular today.

Inasmuch as all of us have a unique personality and individual ways of putting ideas together, our thoughts and speech patterns are not identical. Your sense of timing, manner, even your memory, results from a learned, developed, instinct born out of your individual characteristics. These are very closely interwoven and it is very difficult to separate a person's manner from his timing. By timing we mean the interval between words, sentences, movements, and laughs. Poor timing is exposed by nervousness in rushing lines, putting in too much detail, forgetting important elements and stepping on, or destroying the punch line. In working up and learning a vignette, avoid just looking over material and reading silently to yourself. Instead, read it over and over again, out loud, to get it's verbal feel. You may find yourself stumbling over the sequence in wording; but by repeated practice you will soon find your punch lines, timing and thoughts settling into place and your continuity flowing gracefully. Now is the time to turn to a tape recorder. (Warning: the first time you play back your own voice be ready for a shock. Seldom are we able to assess our delivery in voice patterns accurately.) Just as a mirror or video tape recordings give you a reflection of your physical image — picture of confidence and style — so a recording can reveal voice inflections, timing, pitch level, superfluous words, emphasis, etc. A repeating magazine recorder is an excellent instrument for literally pounding 2, 3, or 5 minute bits into your brain.

Avoid limiting the use of your Sense of Humor to the lunch hour, cocktail hour or party time. Make it a seasoning, not a frosting. Mix it right into the batter of living along with the other ingredients of your personality. Form the habit of pushing your laughter button at every opportunity to simplify, to enlighten, to stimulate your own thought processes and to inspire others.

So . . . release that most rejuvenating of all tonics that stirs your blood, expands your chest, electrifies your nerves and clears away the cobwebs from your brain. Let yourself go, have a ball, but after you've been at it for awhile you might want to check over the dozen don'ts of professional performers and then Test Your Jests, to keep you on the right track and provide the realistic evaluation of your progress. As you master these suggestions and succumb to the inevitable temptation of begetting for posterity your own contribution to the importance of a Sense of Humor, be sure to let me know so I can share in your discoveries.

Just write to:

> **Dr. Herb True**
> **1717 East Colfax Ave.**
> **South Bend, Indiana**
> **46617**
>
> **Telephone: 219/234-2340**

DON'T: . . .

● Limit yourself **just** to material currently making the rounds or collected material from recent TV shows or periodicals . . . also scan back magazines for oldies that others may not have heard lately.

● Tell or use material before large groups until you know and have recited it out loud and have captured it's verbal feel by practicing it in front of a mirror and on casual daily contacts.

● Use a dialect unless you can use it well and in inoffensive manner.

● Pry, strain or force material into a situation that has little connection with your subject, the occasion or the intelligence, experience or occupations of your audience.

● Emphasize material having to do with physical deformities, bodily functions . . . you may succeed in gaining a state of nervous and restrained response, but you'll find listeners looking at others to study their reactions and thus diminish their ability to receive ideas or be inspired.

● Telegraph your blows by announcing you're about to tell a funny.

● Appreciate your own stories to the degree that you **distract** from the material itself, although it's wise to show some signs of enjoyment.

● Step on your punch lines, your applause or laughter — learn to wait.

● Linger over material that has flopped. Instead, fly off the nest if you lay an egg.

TEST YOUR JEST

DID YOU: . . .

● Personalize your humor and make it constructive?

● Reflect a confident, natural, believable manner, show you were having fun infecting others with your sparkle and enthusiasm?

● Speak loud enough to be heard and build up to climaxes?

● Move your head from side to side for change of story characters?

● Remember to use pauses to build and emphasize key words and phrases?

● Really make it **your** material by adapting and relating it to your feeling temperature?

● Have it worked out so perfectly that the plot, climax and punch line developed without stumbling?

● Hit the pay off line hard, pausing for the first titters, building for added response, then stand back and wait for the slow witted to explode?

● Hold a post-mortem with formal or informal appointed personal critic?

DO: Invest in some of the current humor sources available. Write:

Mack McGinnis
448 Mitchner
Indianapolis, Indiana 46219

Robert Orben
Current Comedy
Comedy Center, Inc.
801 Wilmington Trust Building
Wilmington, Delaware 19801

Jokes Un-Ltd.
P.O. Box 69855
Hollywood, California 90069

Funny, Funny World
407 Commercial Center Street
Beverly Hills, California 90210

Quote Magazine
Box 4073 Sta B
Anderson, S. C. 29621

YOUR FUNNYBONE FACTOR

From the time you are born you are measured, ranked and rated. Your height, weight, blood type, pulse, hearing, your I.Q., are all checked against some kind of standards. Yet, there is no valid instrument to rate one of your valuable attributes . . . one that could have more to do with your ability to enjoy and cope with life than any other facet of your personality. So to give you some guidelines on the current status of your "Funnybone Factor", read the following 10 statements. Then, check "Often", "Sometimes", or "Never". It's fun!

	Often	Some-times	Never
1. Do you like to do things "just for the fun of it"?			
2. Do you find yourself searching for a humor break in magazine articles, cartoons, movies, TV programs?			
3. Do you tend to choose, as friends, people whose "Funnybone Factor" you admire?			
4. Do you take pleasure in "Thinking up" a series of funny responses?			
5. Do you treasure memories of humorous things that took place long ago?			
6. Can you wait patiently to tell a joke while somebody else takes the "humor stage"?			
7. Do dull, drab or boring situations challenge you to come up with something to smile about?			
8. Do you ever go out of your way to lighten a friends load by sharing a quip, quote, or a funny happening.			
9. Have you ever found yourself practicing a joke or story in front of a mirror?			
0. Can you really laugh at a joke — even if it's on you?			

To compute your "Funnybone Factor": Score 10 for "Often", 5 for "Sometimes", and 0 for "Never". A score of 75 or more shows your funnybone is limber. 60 to 75 indicates an above-average sense of humor. 40 to 60 indicates your sense of humor is okay, BUT could be better. Below 25 is no laughing matter and may indicate you were weaned on a pickle. If you score 95 — don't kid around! Go right to work as a comedian.

©Dr. Herb True, 1717 E. Colfax, South Bend, Ind. 234-2340

ENJOY
THE WORLD'S GREATEST EDUTAINER
"LIVE"
AT YOUR MEETINGS

When planning your next big convention, banquet, sales rally, business or trade association meeting, remember that you, too, can join the thousands of successful program chairmen who have treated their members, employees, salesmen, distributors, managers, teachers, students and friends to a True-ly exciting, impactful stimulating live program.

Dr. True's professional, colorful, fun filled, graphic presentation will be specially custom-tailored to your audience's specific needs, goals and challenges in the areas of creativity, management, communications, sales, leadership, humor or love. Be among the limited number of audiences who will enjoy and benefit from having Herb True on their program schedule this season.

For availability and specific details on how Dr. True can bring new ideas, put zing, zip, and purposeful enthusiasm into one of your own meetings — seminars — workshops — banquets — or kick-off presentations WRITE or CALL Thelma Howard — program manager — TEAM International, Inc. 1717 E. Colfax, South Bend, Ind. 46617, (219) 234-2340, 233-1757, 234-4795.

120